FINANCIAL SURVIVAL in UNCERTAIN TIMES

Deborah Smith Pegues

HARVEST HOUSE PUBLISHERS

EUGENE, OREGON

Cover by Abris, Veneta, Oregon

FINANCIAL SURVIVAL IN UNCERTAIN TIMES
Copyright © 2009 by Deborah Smith Pegues
Published by Harvest House Publishers
Eugene, Oregon 97402
www.harvesthousepublishers.com

Library of Congress Cataloging-in-Publication Data

Pegues, Deborah Smith, 1950-
Financial survival in uncertain times / Deborah Smith Pegues.
    p. cm.
Rev. ed. of: 30 days to taming your finances.
ISBN 978-0-7369-2727-7 (pbk.)
1. Wealth—Religious aspects—Christianity. 2. Finance, Personal—Religious aspects—Christianity. I. Pegues, Deborah Smith, 1950- 30 days to taming your finances. II. Title.
BR115.W4P45 2009
332.024—dc22

                                                                    2008046154

Printed in the United States of America

        09 10 11 12 13 14 15 16 / BP-NI / 10 9 8 7 6 5 4 3 2 1

CONTENTS

Acknowledgments

Special thanks go to Patrick Harris and Donna Robertson, my brilliant banker friends, who helped me to fully understand the U.S. financial crisis and to put it in terms that will empower every reader.

As always, the moral and technical support provided by my husband, Darnell Pegues, made the project possible. Thanks, Sweetheart.

My editor, Rod Morris, and the Harvest House publishing team are unsurpassed in every way. You guys are the best!

INTRODUCTION
The Worst of Times, the Best of Times

I t was the best of times, it was the worst of times; it was the age of wisdom, it was the age of foolishness…" These introductory words to *A Tale of Two Cities*, Charles Dickens' 1859 historical novel about the French Revolution, could well describe the U.S. economic crisis. Most people view the crisis as the "worst of times"—especially those who had planned to retire but see their nest eggs dwindle, and those who face layoffs, home foreclosures, and other economic woes. Yet, those who trust their God must come to understand that it is the "best of times." It is the best of times to put their faith in action, the best of times to witness God's power to provide, the best of times to model and teach good stewardship to their families, the best of times to stop enabling irresponsible financial behavior, the best of times to show the world the difference that God can make in how a person responds to the vicissitudes of life.

In the following chapters, I will share in easy-to-read laymen's terms the reasons the U.S. finds itself at the center of a global economic tsunami. I will recommend practical strategies that will assure your *financial* survival during uncertain economic times. However, I am keenly aware that your life is not one-dimensional even though money has moved to center stage as the primary preoccupation. Therefore, I will also show you ways to survive and thrive in other areas of your life that are affected when there is a severe economic downturn. These areas include your emotional well-being, your relationships, and your physical health.

A crisis of confidence permeates the global financial systems. More alarming, however, is the crisis of confidence in the Word of our Almighty God. This is evidenced by the increased demand for anti-anxiety medications and the general atmosphere of gloom that pervades the nation. While the U.S. government and its global partners have taken unprecedented actions to restore confidence in the economy, the country, and the banking system, restoring faith in the promises of God can happen only at the individual level.

That's my ultimate goal in writing this book. I want to help you restore or reinforce your confidence in the Word of God. Perhaps one day you too will look back on the crisis and say, "It was the best of times."

Part 1

UNDERSTANDING THE U.S. FINANCIAL CRISIS

1

SUBPRIME LENDING
Borrowers and Bankers Gone Wild

We can lay the blame for the U.S. economic crisis at several doors. The consensus is that subprime lending was the match that lit the fire that threatened to consume the entire world financial system. Further, there is still much debate as to who should be blamed for the fallout of these subprime loans. Since many people remain confused about the meaning and mechanics of such loans, let me attempt to provide a basic understanding.

Understanding the Subprime Debacle

Subprime lending describes the practice of financial institutions providing credit to borrowers deemed "subprime"—that is, those whose credit qualifications are less than ideal or "prime" using traditional criteria. These borrowers include those who have a history of a loan delinquency or default, those with a recorded bankruptcy, or those with limited debt experience. Further, their FICO credit scores (explained below) usually fall below a certain level.

Historically, banks made home loans based upon three primary factors: creditworthiness, cash flow, and collateral.

Creditworthiness is determined by the borrower having an acceptable credit history as measured by a FICO score. FICO stands for Fair Isaac Corporation, the entity that came up with the methodology which reduces your credit history to a three-digit number ranging from 350 to 850 with ratings as follows:

- *Excellent:* 750 and over
- *Very Good:* 720 to 750
- *Acceptable:* 660 to 720
- *Uncertain:* 620 to 660
- *High Risk:* less than 620

Most lenders, or any entity extending credit, view the FICO score as the primary predictor of future credit performance. During the subprime lending craze, loans were extended to borrowers with scores below 660 (albeit at high rates), increasing the risk of default. (I'll explain the nuances of the FICO score in chapter 8, "Master Your Debts.")

Cash flow is simply a measure of your ability to make the mortgage payment based upon your income and existing expenses. Traditionally, lenders used an average qualifying ratio of 28 percent/36 percent. This meant that your total mortgage payment (including principal, interest, property taxes, and mortgage insurance if required) could not exceed 28 percent of your gross income. When added together with all other contractual debt (auto loans, credit cards) the total (including the new mortgage) was not to exceed 36 percent of the gross income of all parties included in the loan application.

One of the most irresponsible concessions lenders made was to qualify borrowers based on "stated income." Yes, you read right—income as stated by the borrower. The lender made no effort to verify the annual income by reviewing tax returns, 1099s, W-2 earnings statements, or other means of confirmation. The only documentation was what the borrower "stated" his income to be. This was a particular advantage for self-employed people who had usually met strong resistance from lenders in proving their income. Some jokingly referred to such loans as "liar loans."

Subprime lenders also began to offer "teaser rates" or special terms that served to lower the payments during the first few years of the loan. For example, assume that Larry the laborer obtained a $300,000, 30-year loan at 4 percent interest-only for the first three years. The loan agreement further states that after three years, he would start to pay principal and 6.5 percent interest. Now, Larry and his stay-at-home wife, Lucy, are happy. Their loan payment (excluding property taxes and insurance) is only $1,000 per month for the first three years. Larry earns a fairly stable income of $48,000 annually ($4,000/month) at a local construction firm. The terms of his loan allowed him to easily meet the lender's relaxed qualifying ratios, which required total gross income of about three times the monthly payment, or $3,000 per month.

To boot, the lender offered even more generous terms. They told Larry that his total debt commitments (including his mortgage) could go up to 45 percent or more of his gross income (versus the traditional 36 percent). This worked out well since Larry and Lucy both had outstanding auto loans on their two gas-guzzling SUVs with combined payments totaling over $600/month. Larry obtained the loan in his name only because Lucy's credit was totally shot.

At the end of the three years, Larry's mortgage loan resets, and he finds himself responsible for principal and 6.5 percent interest payments on the $300,000 loan for the 27-year remaining term. His principal and interest payment is now a whopping $1,966, almost double the $1,000 he had grown accustomed to paying. His take-home pay is only $2,800 after taxes and various other deductions. He has two years remaining to pay on the SUVs. Larry is now committed to monthly payments of $2,566 ($1,966 new mortgage + $600 auto loans). He will have less than $250 for all other household expenses.

Larry now faces a financial crisis.

What we saw at the epicenter of the U.S. financial crisis were millions of loans that reached the interest rate reset date only to find that the borrower could not afford the higher payment due to inadequate income, higher food and fuel prices, and a number of other unfavorable economic factors.

Collateral is the value of property pledged as security for a loan. In the old days, a 10 percent down payment was the norm (the ideal was 20 percent), and every would-be homeowner saved toward it. Lenders knew that with such a big personal investment on the line, a homeowner was less likely to throw in the towel and walk away from a home when facing a financial crisis.

Some government-guaranteed programs allowed a 3 percent down payment for those who would have otherwise been denied access to credit and the American dream. However, during the subprime craze, many lenders waived down payment requirements altogether and made loans that even exceeded the market values of the homes. It was not uncommon to see ads touting loans up to 125 percent of the current market value in areas where homes were appreciating at a rate of 15 percent annually. The thinking was that real estate values would continue to increase at that same rate well into the future. The logic that a house in a market appreciating at 15 percent annually would be worth 30 percent more in two years seemed to hold water at the time. So, even if the borrower ran into financial problems, he could simply sell the house at a profit if necessary.

When we peek in on Larry and Lucy, we learn that their house is now worth only $225,000, and Larry is facing a layoff due to the downturn in the housing market. Looks like the bank and Larry were wrong in their assumptions.

Across the United States, this scenario was repeated by millions. Bankers and borrowers had gone wild and now had to face new realities as market prices dropped by up to 50 percent in many areas, leaving millions of under-collateralized loans.

Why didn't Larry and Lucy do the math and determine if they would ever be able to pay $1,966 in principal and interest? Why didn't the bank do the math? Why was everyone so shortsighted? Perhaps the mortgage brokers were too busy being salesmen? Perhaps the desire for bigger and better overwhelmed Larry and Lucy?

Everybody was at fault.

In the next chapter, we'll look at what happened to Larry's loan and at the fallout from this fiasco.

2

Mortgage-Backed Securities
American Dream Turned Global Nightmare

The day that Larry the laborer obtained his $300,000 subprime mortgage, the bank also offered him and Lucy a home equity line of credit to complete the finishing touches on their dream home. To their credit, caution prevailed and they drew down only $3,000, which they paid off after the first year. For now, they are happy campers.

Let's see what life looks like for the lender.

In the old days, the bank would have made the loan to Larry and kept it on their books until he paid it off. This was called "warehousing" the loan. Of course, the bank made mortgage and other loans from the deposits it had accepted from its customers in the form of checking or savings accounts, certificates of deposit, and so forth. However, there were lots of Larrys pursuing the American dream. Being consumers at heart, the bank customers did not deposit enough in their accounts to provide a continuous supply of capital to all the borrowers applying for loans. The bank decided to sell the loan to the "secondary market" at a profit in order to replenish its capital and make more loans.

It retained the right to collect Larry's payment, so he never knew the difference.

Enter Fannie Mae and Freddie Mac.

The Lowdown on Fannie Mae and Freddie Mac

The national housing market collapsed during the Great Depression. In response, President Franklin Roosevelt established the Federal National Mortgage Association (nicknamed Fannie Mae) in 1938 as part of his "New Deal" solution to the economic crisis. The objective was to provide local banks with federal money to finance mortgages to increase home ownership and to assure affordable housing. This was the birth of the secondary mortgage market. In the secondary market, Fannie Mae was able to borrow money from foreign investors at low interest rates because such loans were backed by the full faith and credit of the U.S. government. Passing a portion of the savings on to borrowers via the local banks created a win-win situation.

For over 30 years, Fannie Mae monopolized the secondary market. In 1968, President Lyndon Johnson removed it from the federal budget and privatized it. Now investors other than the government would bankroll its operation, freeing the federal budget of funds needed for the Vietnam War.

To end Fannie Mae's monopoly and in the American spirit of free enterprise, Congress chartered the Federal Home Loan Mortgage Corporation (nicknamed Freddie Mac) in 1970 with the same mandate as Fannie Mae. Both companies are publically traded, shareholder-owned entities. They are Government Sponsored Enterprises (GSE) but not agencies of the U.S. government. Therefore, there is no annual budget appropriation for their operations (as there had been for Fannie Mae before it was privatized in 1968). They are different from a regular publically traded company in some key aspects:

- They are federally chartered and are subject to congressional mandates.
- They have a several-billion dollar line of credit with the U.S. government.
- A portion of the board of directors is appointed by the president of the U.S.
- They are exempt from state and local income taxes.
- They are exempt from filing with the Securities and Exchange Commission.
- Their securities are not *officially* backed by the full faith and credit of the U.S. government.

Fannie and Freddie are not direct lenders; their objective is to make sure that banks have a steady supply of capital to make home loans. Think of them as the "second" stop for the majority of the conventional and conforming mortgage loans in the U.S. They buy the loans from the bank and thus provide the bank with the capital to make more loans. They keep some of the loans in their portfolio; others they bundle and sell to investors as mortgage-backed securities (MBS) or bonds. Before they can sell to investors, they must get a rating from a securities rating service indicating that the bonds are "investment grade," that is, high enough quality for a prudent investor to purchase them. (Analysts at Moody's Investors Service, Standard & Poor's, and Fitch Ratings had doubts about many of the mortgage-backed securities they rated, but they gave them a thumbs-up because it was so lucrative to do so, according to documents released by a U.S. House panel [http://oversight.house.gov/story.asp?ID=2250].)

Fannie and Freddie are the owners or guarantors of over half of the $12 trillion in mortgages in the U.S. and the biggest issuers of MBSs in the world. Thus, you can see how critical these entities are on the national and world scene.

Let's assume that Fannie Mae now has Larry and Lucy's mortgage. They take the mortgage and combine it with similar mortgages and package it as a debt security (a bond) where investors (foreign governments, pension funds, etc.) are paid interest from the interest Larry and millions of other homeowners pay on their loans. All goes well until Larry and others run into trouble and cannot make their payments.

Investors, including the company managing your retirement fund, cannot get paid on the bonds and therefore can't make payouts to the people on whose behalf they have invested.

There is now a domino effect. The investors who purchased the bonds from Fannie or Freddie don't trust that they are a good source for investment, so they stop buying their mortgage-backed securities. When they stop buying the securities, Fannie and Freddie cannot provide capital to the banks. If capital is in short supply, the banks simply cannot make mortgage loans. If people can't get mortgages, homes won't be sold and builders can't get capital to build new houses. Workers will have to be laid off in all of the related trades. Layoffs mean that more people cannot afford to pay their existing mortgages. (If you are still confused by all of this, perhaps the chart in appendix 1, "The Mortgage Cycle," will clarify the flow of mortgage capital.)

This discussion of defaults on the mortgages that have been sold as securities also applies to investment banks that purchased mortgage bonds from lending institutions and even from Fannie and Freddie. Many commercial banks and foreign governments (especially China) also heavily invested in the mortgage bonds of Fannie and Freddie.

Fannie and Freddie's response to their cash-flow dilemma was to go out into the credit market in mid-2008 and try to raise money to make good on the bond payments. However, they were not able to do so. Neither foreign governments nor financial institutions would invest in one of the most important members of Fortune 500 powerhouses.

Realizing that the whole financial system would crash without quick intervention, the government stepped in and put both companies into conservatorship (this means the government will do the managing from now on) and invested $100 billion of additional capital in each entity. This $200 billion bailout was not part of the controversial $700 billion bailout I will discuss in the next chapter.

So if you want to place blame for the U.S. financial fiasco, fingers could point in several directions: The Federal Reserve could have stopped the irresponsible lending practices that fueled the subprime mortgage market; the Securities and Exchange Commission (SEC) could have insisted on stricter standards for the agencies that rated the safety of the securities; Fannie Mae and Freddie Mac should not have relaxed their criteria for the types of loans they would purchase or guarantee; the banks could have shown more concern for their customers and not pushed the unaffordable loans; borrowers could have faced reality and walked away from mortgages their budgets could not accommodate.

All of these and more played a role in the fiasco.

3

GOVERNMENT BAILOUT
Bad or Biblical?

The old adage that there is nothing new under the sun still rings true. Since the beginning of time, economic crises have come and gone. The role of government in addressing and minimizing the impact of these troubled times are depicted in the early pages of the Bible. Indeed many of the economic crises recorded in the Bible resulted from the ruling king's own policies. For example, Egypt experienced many plagues, including a crop-destroying locust infestation, because Pharaoh stubbornly refused to release the Israelites from bondage (Exodus 10). In another instance, a three-year drought devastated Israel's economy because King Ahab and his evil wife, Jezebel, encouraged worship of the idol Baal (1 Kings 16–17).

Perhaps the most unforgettable economic crisis was the seven-year drought in Egypt that followed seven years of unprecedented prosperity (Genesis 41–47). God warned Pharaoh of the impending downturn through a dream that none of the local magicians or wise men could interpret. However, the king's butler remembered that Joseph, a falsely charged Hebrew slave, had interpreted his dream while they were in jail together. So the king summoned Joseph from the prison to interpret the dream. Joseph not only interpreted the dream, but also recommended a plan that would mitigate the impact of the seven years of famine that were sure to come. Seeing that God was obviously with Joseph, Pharaoh decided that he was the man to lead the government's response. In a single day, Joseph went from being a prisoner to being the prime minister and was granted broad authority second only to Pharaoh.

By the time the famine set in, Joseph had systematically stored 20 percent of the food harvest in government warehouses during each of the years of prosperity. Crop failures began to abound and people were on the brink of starvation.

> So when all the land of Egypt was famished, the people
> cried to Pharaoh for bread. Then Pharaoh said to all
> the Egyptians, "Go to Joseph; whatever he says to you,
> do." The famine was over all the face of the earth,
> and Joseph opened all the storehouses and sold to the
> Egyptians. And the famine became severe in the land
> of Egypt. So all countries came to Joseph in Egypt to
> buy grain, because the famine was severe in all lands
> (Genesis 41:55-57).

Pretty soon, the people ran out of money and more government intervention was required for survival. During the famine, Joseph accepted people's livestock in exchange for food, relocated many to the inner city to facilitate the government's assistance program, and purchased all the land in Egypt from landowners and made them sharecroppers.

> Then Joseph said to the people, "Indeed I have bought
> you and your land this day for Pharaoh. Look, here

is seed for you, and you shall sow the land. And it shall come to pass in the harvest that you shall give one-fifth to Pharaoh. Four-fifths shall be your own, as seed for the field and for your food, for those of your households and as food for your little ones" (Genesis 47:23-24).

No one complained of too much government intervention; all were grateful for the economic relief. "So they said, 'You have saved our lives; let us find favor in the sight of my lord, and we will be Pharaoh's servants'" (v. 25).

Socialism Versus Capitalism: God's Choice

I would do you a disservice were I to remain silent about which form of economic structure the Bible supports: socialism or capitalism. In light of the government's bailout or temporary takeover of key corporations, many pundits and politicians have expressed their grave concern about the U.S. becoming a socialist society. Others are equally concerned that unchecked capitalism has led to the worst financial crisis since the Great Depression.

Socialism in its purest form seeks to achieve economic equality for all by having the government take the wealth of the rich, without their consent, and redistribute it to the needy. Thus, private ownership and control of personal wealth are not allowed. Proponents of socialism cite the early church as a model of socialism using the following passages of Scripture:

> Now all who believed were together, and had all things in common, and sold their possessions and goods, and divided them among all, as anyone had need (Acts 2:44-45).

> Nor was there anyone among them who lacked; for all
> who were possessors of lands or houses sold them, and
> brought the proceeds of the things that were sold, and
> laid them at the apostles' feet; and they distributed to
> each as anyone had need (Acts 4:34-35).

This was not a *redistribution* of wealth by the government but a *voluntary distribution* from the "haves"—via the church—to the "have nots." Socialism takes away the power of choice regarding how benevolent the rich will be toward the poor. Therefore, the distributions by the early church can best be described as *responsible capitalism*.

The essence of *capitalism* is that profit is the important factor when decisions are made in the affairs of men.

Christians who argue in favor of capitalism cite the story Jesus told of the master who gave three employees certain "talents" or sums of money to invest on his behalf while he went on an extended trip (Matthew 25:14-30). The amount he gave to each was based upon that employee's ability to manage. Sure enough, the two employees who were given the most doubled their investment, and they were commended by the master and given greater authority. The one who received the smallest sum didn't even put his master's money in an interest-bearing bank account but buried it until the master's return. The master was quite displeased with the non-enterprising servant and strongly reprimanded him.

> "But his lord answered and said to him, 'You wicked
> and lazy servant...you ought to have deposited my
> money with the bankers, and at my coming I would
> have received back my own with interest. So take the
> talent from him, and give it to him who has ten tal-
> ents'" (Matthew 25:26-28).

Under capitalism in its purest form, it is survival of the "financial" fittest. Ironically, socialism needs capitalism to exist; after all, somebody has to make the money, whether it is forcefully redistributed by the government or voluntarily distributed by the owners of capital.

So while the Bible endorses private ownership, it does not promote socialism or capitalism in their extreme forms. Those with resources are simply admonished to help the less fortunate. "But whoever has this world's goods, and sees his brother in need, and shuts up his heart from him, how does the love of God abide in him?" (1 John 3:17).

The U.S. $700 Billion Bailout

The U.S. effort to stabilize its economy pales in comparison to the biblical bailout previously discussed. The Emergency Economic Stabilization Act of 2008 (EESA) signed into law on October 3, 2008 by President George W. Bush was just the beginning of the drastic measures needed to address the financial crisis. The controversial bill was widely opposed by several members of both political parties, some economists, educators, talk-show commentators, and taxpayers. However, when the dust settled, everyone agreed that something had to be done to reestablish confidence in the nation's financial and credit systems or they would have completely collapsed.

Since the average person did not quite understand the contents and ramifications of the bailout legislation, here is my edited and annotated version of the summary that appears on the government's website (http://banking.senate.gov/public/_files/latestversionEESA Summary.pdf). My brief explanations may not encompass all the nuances of the program; however, my goal is to provide only a general understanding. At least this knowledge may mitigate some anger and frustration. The objectives of the bill were as follows:

Stabilizing the Economy: The law provides up to $700 billion to the Secretary of the Treasury to *buy* troubled mortgages and other assets that spoil the balance sheets of financial institutions. (These mortgages can be resold to investors.) Accounting mark-to-market rules dictate these institutions must mark down troubled loans to the current *market values* of the properties rather than the amount of the outstanding loans. In the case of Larry and Lucy, whom we discussed in previous chapters, their loan balance was $300,000 but their house is now worth only $225,000. The institution holding their mortgage as an investment must record a $75,000 loss on its books and show a $225,000 asset. This write down has now reduced available capital; thus, less credit is available.

Credit is vital to a strong and stable economy. Without the cash infusion from the government, it would be difficult for working families, small businesses, and other companies to access credit. This isn't just about bailing out the fat cats or helping irresponsible borrowers; it's about freeing up the money supply to keep the lending cycle flowing for consumer mortgages, retailers, and manufacturers. Understand that it will not help the value of your home if a house next door has been repossessed and sits vacant because potential buyers cannot get financing.

Rather than authorizing the disbursement of all the funds at once, the bailout legislation gives the Treasury $250 billion immediately, then requires the president to certify that another $100 billion is needed. The disbursement of the final $350 billion is subject to congressional disapproval.

Homeownership Preservation: The EESA requires the Treasury to modify troubled loans—many of which resulted from shady lending practices—wherever possible to help American families keep their homes. It also directs other federal agencies to modify loans that they own or control.

Taxpayer Protection: In response to the cry of taxpayers that they should not be expected to pay for Wall Street's mistakes, the legislation requires companies that sell some of their bad assets to the government to provide warrants (options to purchase stock) so that the government (and thus taxpayers) will benefit from any future growth these companies may experience as a result of participation in this program. The legislation also requires the president to submit legislation that would recoup from the financial institutions any losses to taxpayers resulting from this program.

No Windfalls for Executives: Executives who made bad decisions should not be allowed to dump their troubled assets on the government and then walk away with millions of dollars in bonuses. Thus, companies who participate in this program will lose certain tax benefits and, in some cases, must limit executive pay. In addition, the legislation limits "golden parachutes" (special bonuses or compensation paid when an executive is terminated). It also requires that unearned bonuses be returned.

Strong Oversight: The Treasury must report on the use of the bailout funds and the progress in addressing the crisis. EESA also establishes an oversight board so that the Treasury cannot act in an arbitrary manner. It also establishes a special inspector general to protect against waste, fraud, and abuse.

The U.S. government is hopeful that a significant amount of the $700 billion will be recouped when the economy rebounds. This is a reasonable expectation in light of past experience. The government bailed out the Chrysler Corporation in 1980 by providing $1.5

billion in loan guarantees to save the company from insolvency. By 1983, seven years earlier than the scheduled deadline, Chrysler had paid back the guaranteed loans. The corporation bought back the 14.4 million stock warrants given to the government in exchange for the loan guarantee. Because Chrysler's finances had improved and its stock had bounced back—it reported $1.7 billion in profits for the second quarter of 1984—the government netted a profit of more than $660 million from its bailout investment (www.propublica.org/special/government-bailouts).

While we all prefer unregulated freedom, we have seen the often negative impact on society when the government takes a hands-off approach (example, exorbitant interest rates on credit cards). Fortunately, the U.S. is a democracy in which the two major political parties keep the government from going overboard in regulation or deregulation. Yes, all taxpayers will eventually feel the pinch of the bailout in higher taxes, reduced government services, reduced credit limits, and other measures. However, we must watch our attitudes as God's children toward those we think do not *deserve* to benefit from the bailout due to their greed or irresponsible decisions. Jesus reminded His followers that God "makes His sun rise on the evil and on the good, and sends rain on the just and on the unjust" (Matthew 5:45).

Let's keep extending grace.

Part 2

TEN STRATEGIES FOR NAVIGATING FINANCIAL UNCERTAINTY

4

KNOW WHERE YOU STAND

Y ou are here" were the first words I saw on a huge map as I entered the Las Vegas mall. As simple as it sounds, this was a strategic piece of information. I had come to the mall to purchase something from a certain store. I needed to assess my position before I could start on the path to my desired destination. Otherwise, I would have wandered aimlessly, possibly become distracted by the merchandise in other stores, and may have never reached my goal.

Dealing with our finances works much the same way. Many of us put forth a lot of effort but end up spinning our wheels because we don't stop to take stock of where we are. It reminds me of the story of the commercial airline pilot who, during a cross-country flight, made the following announcement: "Ladies and gentlemen, I have good news and bad news. First, the good news. Due to favorable wind currents, we are able to go faster than usual. The bad news is that our navigation equipment is broken, and we don't know where we are!"

We must determine where we are before we start to pursue the path to our financial destiny. To answer the question "Where am I?" we must look at two aspects of our finances: (1) what we own and what we owe, and (2) what we make and where it goes.

You can determine the first aspect, "What I Own and What I Owe," by completing what is often called a Statement of Financial Position or a Balance Sheet, which summarizes your assets and liabilities. (See the form in Appendix 2.) Your assets will consist of everything you own that has value, including bank accounts, paintings, jewelry, furs, collectible loans due from others, cash value of whole-life insurance policies, and so forth. You will list cars and real estate, even if you are still paying on them. Caution! Many people erroneously include the amount of insurance coverage on their term-life policy. This is not an asset that you can redeem for cash today. It becomes an asset only to your heirs when you pass away.

Under your liabilities you will include installment debt, credit card balances, personal loans, home mortgage, and everything you owe. We will deal with how to manage your debt in a later chapter. For now, we're just going to figure out how much you owe. Don't go ostrich on me by sticking your head in the sand. Face your reality. Get your credit card bills and write down each outstanding balance. If you are pretty much maxed out on all your cards, don't worry; you have lots of company. Besides, I'm going to show you how to dig yourself out of the debt pit.

For the second aspect, "What I Make and Where It Goes," you will need to do a little more work. This information is summarized on a Statement of Income and Expenditures, often referred to as an Income Statement. (See the form in Appendix 3.) Here you list all of your take-home income from various sources. You will list your expenditures in two basic categories: fixed and discretionary.

The fixed expenditures are those that will continue to occur each month whether you have income or not, such as your rent or mortgage payment, car payment, insurance, and so forth. Discretionary expenses are the ones you can control from month to month. If your finances are out of control, you may not be aware of how much you're spending on discretionary expenses, such as food, personal grooming, entertainment, and so forth. So, for at least a couple of weeks (a month is preferred), write down every discretionary expenditure you make. To make this a little easier for you, I have included in Appendix 4 a worksheet to help you monitor your spending. You can summarize the spending categories later.

This process may seem cumbersome, but it's going to pay off. By making this short-term investment of time to see where your money is going, you'll be armed with information that will allow you to control your spending in the long term. Besides, the Balance Sheet and Income Statement may be required when it comes time to negotiate with lenders to reduce your debts. So knuckle down and invest the time to see where you stand.

Be completely honest here. Some people sabotage this process by listing what they think they *should* be spending rather than what they actually spend. It's extremely important to complete this exercise because it reveals your real financial priorities, not what you claim they are. If I found your checkbook, I could conclude from reviewing it what your spending priorities are. So just note the real deal. You will probably be shocked to see where your money is going.

Pay particular attention to the amounts you spend for eating out, snacks, newspapers, and so forth. I was taken aback when my husband, Darnell, and I went through this process a couple of years ago and saw how much we were spending on eating out and for recreation. My immediate response was to cut everything out, but that's not necessarily the best solution. Even during times of uncertainty, there's a place for doing what we can to maintain a good quality of life.

5

DEAL WITH YOUR
SPENDING MOTIVATORS

I have long maintained that every spending decision is tied to emotions, temptations, or other psychological factors. Even responsible decisions find their roots in the need for such things as safety and security. The Scriptures sternly admonish,

> Do not love this world nor the things it offers you, for when you love the world, you do not have the love of the Father in you. For the world offers only a craving for physical pleasure, a craving for everything we see, and pride in our achievements and possessions. These are not from the Father, but are from this world (1 John 2:15-16 NLT).

Herein lies the root cause of the U.S. financial crisis: greed, the lust for everything we see, and the quest for validation of our worth. I have found that teaching the mechanics and how-tos of budgeting and financial planning really doesn't offer a permanent solution to a person's spending problem. I have to get to the core issues that drive that person's spending habits.

Emotional spending is first cousin to emotional eating. In both cases, a feeling inside cries out for satisfaction. Spending to pacify an emotion is like getting an anesthetic but never having the surgery. You get temporary relief, but the problem remains.

Let's look at a few emotions that may cause you to want to spend outside of your budget and a strategy for dealing with each.

Anger

If you peel the onion of why you are angry, at the core you may find that you are angry with yourself for tolerating someone's bad behavior, for not speaking up, for putting yourself at risk, or for a host of other reasons. Before you run to the mall, get in touch with why you are feeling the way you do and confront the people involved. If face-to-face is not possible, then write a letter expressing how you feel about what has happened. Ask God to give you the words and the wisdom to be direct, honest, and godly in your approach.

Boredom

I talked to a middle-aged single woman the other day who had maxed out her cards. When I asked her how that had happened, she said, "I don't have a husband. I guess I'm just bored." The best way to deal with boredom is to invest time in meaningful activity that either moves you toward your goals or makes life better for someone else. Take a class to enhance your skills or knowledge. Sign up with a group to visit nursing homes, hospitals, orphanages, and shelters. Go alone if you have to. It is so fulfilling to help others not be bored. Plant what you want to reap, and most of all, stay away from TV and Internet shopping, which make it so easy to indulge your fantasies.

Depression

I know I'm treading on sensitive ground here, but if you are depressed, it may be because you have focused all of your attention on how things are affecting you. You have become the center of your world. If you would dare to step out of the spotlight and shine it on someone else, you would find amazing results. See the suggestions above for possible activities that may refocus your attention. At the same time, I encourage you to seek medical attention to determine if your depression is caused by a chemical imbalance or other medical reasons.

Low Self-Esteem

When you feel unsure of your inherent worth, you may find yourself buying things that will impress others of your value. This can take the form of cars, clothes, jewelry, and other trappings. Some people can't afford to buy the real deal, so they buy knock-offs of designer merchandise hoping that no one will know the difference. They give the phrase "dress to impress" a whole new meaning. If you find yourself with this mind-set, admit it and stop living the lie. Start to slowly abandon out-of-reach purchases and begin to spend at a level you can afford. Honor intangibles that you bring to the table, such as a sense of humor, integrity, perseverance, and so forth. Don't be like Haman, the insecure Persian official who needed the king's horse, the king's robe, and association with a noble prince to feel honored (Esther 6:7-9).

Frustration

Disappointment over thwarted plans or desires can send you running for the mall, especially when you haven't embraced the truth that no man can thwart God's plans for your life. Listen up. If God wants a certain situation to come to pass, nobody can stop it. Perhaps He is working out in you something of more eternal value. Release it to Him. Father knows best.

Desire for Respect

I know firsthand that you will tend to garner more respect in certain social settings if you look prosperous. Society defines success by how you look, what you drive, and other trappings. That's a reality that you cannot change. However, you can decide to set your own parameters on how far you are willing to go to enjoy that kind of social clout and remain your authentic self. I have high respect for people who refuse to follow that path and instead forge their own individuality.

Easy Credit Pressure

Go into any major department store and a clerk will likely try to get you to open an account on the spot and reward you with a discount. Even if you already have a store charge card, they will offer you a discount if you charge that day's purchase. Here's my secret for responding to this pressure. Say, "No, thank you" if you don't already have a store card. If you do and the discount is just too good to resist, charge the item and go immediately to the customer service or collections department and pay it off—yes, even before you leave the store. I've actually paid off my bill at the same checkout stand right after they rang up my sale and gave me a discount for using the store's credit card. Mission accomplished.

Temptation

You can often have the best intentions but allow the media, family, friends, or others to tempt you to spend unwisely. I'm pretty frugal, so I don't consider myself an emotional spender. However, after I've worked really hard on a project and finally finish it, I often reward myself by buying something.

I spoke at a women's conference on the East Coast recently, and afterward some of the ladies offered to take me to see their beautiful, upscale mall. I could not believe that I let three shopaholics talk me into buying a pair of pumps that cost more—even on sale—than I would ever pay for three pairs of shoes. Oh, the pressure from my cohorts!

"You work hard."

"You deserve them."

"They will last forever."

"Oprah wears this brand."

I succumbed. I think it was the Oprah comment that sold me. It gave me celebrity status, a common trick advertisers use.

I charged the shoes on my credit card for convenience and paid the bill in full when it arrived. I still wonder what it would have felt like if I had shelled out hard cash for that purchase. The problem with using a credit card is that you don't immediately experience the painful consequence of parting with the cash.

The moral of this story is to shop alone (or with a frugal friend) and pay with cash. Studies show that you always spend more when you use a credit card.

The most critical question you should ask yourself is, "What is the best way to deal with this emotion?" Then you can address the issue of the item you are about to buy. Do I need it? Is it outside of my spending plan? Does it advance the ball down my financial court?

I know I've only touched the tip of the iceberg in listing the emotions that motivate spending. However, it's incumbent upon you to do your own soul searching and to get real about what attitudes, self-limiting beliefs, and negative emotions keep you from soaring in your finances.

6

DEVELOP YOUR
FINANCIAL ROAD MAP

Your overall financial vision, as God's child, should be to be an excellent manager of the resources God entrusts to you. "Write the vision and make it plain on tablets, that he may run who reads it" (Habakkuk 2:2). I can guarantee you that if you don't write down your vision for your finances, the chances of it coming to pass are slim to none.

Your *goals,* versus your *vision,* are the long-term and short-term achievements you plan to accomplish to make your vision come to pass. Your goals should emanate from the heart of God rather than from your fleshly nature or desires. So before you etch your vision and goals in stone, don't forget to submit them to God. Invest some time in prayer alone and with another person you know to be sensitive to God's voice.

> Commit to the LORD whatever you do,
> and your plans will succeed.
>
> (PROVERBS 16:3 NIV)

Don't make the mistake of putting forth your money and efforts only to find that you are climbing the wrong ladder to success. I am frequently reminded of the story of godly King Jehoshaphat, who invested hard work and capital into a shipbuilding venture that never got off the ground.

> Near the end of his life, King Jehoshaphat of Judah made an alliance with King Ahaziah of Israel, who was a very wicked man. Together they built a fleet of trading ships at the port of Ezion-geber. Then Eliezer son of Dodavahu from Mareshah prophesied against Jehoshaphat. He said, "Because you have allied yourself with King Ahaziah, the LORD will destroy your work." So the ships met with disaster and never put out to sea (2 Chronicles 20:35-37 NLT).

Whether written or not, plans are guaranteed to fail if they do not line up with the will of God. "'Destruction is certain for my rebellious children,' says the LORD. 'You make plans that are contrary to my will. You weave a web of plans that are not from my Spirit, thus piling up your sins'" (Isaiah 30:1 NLT).

Once you get the green light from God, write down your overall vision and your goals. Written goals give energy. The more you read them, the more energized you become toward them. You need to divide your goals into two categories: short-term and long-term. The short-term goals represent what you'd like to achieve within the next three years. Long-term goals are your desires for four to ten years from now. Prioritize each one according to its importance to you and indicate a specific date by which you plan to accomplish the goal. *A goal without a due date is just a wish.*

Sure, you'll get to it someday. "Someday" is the date by which everybody plans to get in shape, pay off credit cards, apologize for bad behavior, and complete a host of other positive projects or dreaded necessities. Someday is no day. Every goal must have a milestone date by which something will happen that gets you closer to the end result. There is a line in the popular hymn "Yield Not to Temptation" that says, "Each victory will help you some other to win." These interim victories keep you motivated to keep going forward.

Where to?

Whether your goal is to survive or to soar during uncertain times, you need a plan of action. "Good planning and hard work lead to prosperity" (Proverbs 21:5 NLT). Auguste Nélaton, the great French surgeon, once said, "If I had four minutes in which to perform an operation on which a life depended, I would take one minute to consider how best to do it." The adage may have become trite, but it is still true: *If you fail to plan, then you plan to fail.*

Now that you have determined where you stand, you are ready to chart your course—not to riches, but to financial freedom. Financial freedom is simply being free from anxiety about financial matters. Developing and implementing an effective spending plan—I dare not use the word *budget*—involves four major actions: (1) determining where you are currently spending the money, (2) evaluating your spending in light of your financial goals, (3) identifying and eliminating behaviors or circumstances that lead to unnecessary spending, and (4) monitoring your ongoing expenditures to make sure they are consistent with your financial goals. You completed the first step in the previous chapter, so you are now poised for steps 2 through 4.

Here is a list of possible short-term and long-term goals to get you started:

Short-Term Goals:

I will establish an emergency fund to cover one month of living expenses by _____.

I will start a part-time business by _____.

I will eliminate all credit card debt by _____.

I will take a dream vacation to _____ by _____.

I will save $_____ to begin phase one of my kitchen remodeling project by _____.

I will move into my own apartment by _____.

I will complete my college degree by _____.

Other:_____

Long-Term Goals:

I will save $_____ for my child's college education by _____.

I will purchase a home by _____.

I will invest at least $_____ in my retirement fund by _____.

Other:_____

Even if you miss your targeted due date, awareness of a deadline will give momentum to your effort. Just keep moving forward. You don't have to think of a zillion goals right now. Just start with one. Succeeding at one thing can ignite your hope. Write or type it in large letters. Start with the words, "By the grace of God, I will _____ by _____." Be emphatic. "I will" is more energizing than "I'm going to try" or "I hope to." To stay accountable and true to your goals, prudently share them with someone who has demonstrated his support. Give him a copy and permission to monitor your progress.

Before you chisel your goals in stone, it's important to ask yourself, "Do these goals represent my vision or someone else's vision for me?" For example, "Do I really want to go back and get that college degree, even though I'm making good money, or am I just pacifying my spouse's desire for more social status?"

If your goals are not God-inspired and ones that you can pursue with all your might, your motivation may wane and you may find yourself resenting the inevitable struggles—as well as the person who pushed you into them—when things get tough along the way. There are endless stories of people who went to college and majored in subjects they had little interest in, but they did so to pacify pushy parents. In many cases they are in unfulfilling, high-paying jobs and feel trapped because of their upscale lifestyles and corresponding financial obligations. Do the soul-searching before you even start.

You must be excited about the benefits of reaching the goal. Jesus was "willing to die a shameful death on the cross because of the joy he knew would be his afterward. Now he is seated in the place of highest honor beside God's throne in heaven" (Hebrews 12:2 NLT). When Jesus died on the cross, He had achieved His vision. He said, "It is finished" (John 19:30). Mission accomplished.

Whatever goals you set, your strategy must be designed to take you in that direction. For example, if you have a long-term goal of saving enough money for a down payment on a house, know that you are sabotaging it when you continue to purchase designer clothes on your credit card each month. Your goal should be to eliminate as much credit card debt as possible. You will never get to the West if you follow a route to the East. Again, I challenge you to look at your goals and decide if you are ready to pursue a plan that will get you to where you want to be.

Developing a Spending Plan

Because each person's financial situation is unique, there is no cookie-cutter budget that fits all. How you set up your plan is largely dependent on where you live, your marital status, and other personal circumstances. Below are some general guidelines for how a typical plan would look for a person who is trying to bring his finances under control. The example assumes a gross annual salary of $36,000.

Sample Spending Plan	%	Monthly	Annually*
Gross Income	100.00%	$3,000	$36,000
Shelter	28.00%	840	10,080
Tithes/Offerings/Gifts	11.00%	330	3,960
Short-Term Savings	3.00%	90	1,080
Long-Term Savings/ Investments/Retirement	3.00%	90	1,080
Debt Reduction/Other	4.00%	120	1,440
Insurance	2.00%	60	720
Transportation	12.00%	360	4,320
Food	13.00%	390	4,680
Recreation/Social Life	5.00%	150	1,800
Subtotal Before Taxes	81.00%	2,430	29,160
Social Security/Medicare Taxes	7.65%	230	2,754
Federal/State/Other Taxes	11.35%	340	4,086
Total Expenditures	100.00%	3,000	36,000

*For ease of understanding, these numbers have been rounded.

You will need to consider each line item as it relates to your circumstances. For example, if you are married, have a roommate, or live at home with your parents, your Shelter costs may be a lot lower. You will then want to allocate some of the excess funds from this area to another category. Keep in mind that your Shelter costs include everything you spend money on to live in your dwelling: utilities, phone, maintenance, and so forth.

As you reviewed the sample budget above, I'm sure you noted that the Tithe, Offerings, and Gifts category appears to take a significant chunk out of your available funds. In a subsequent chapter, we'll look at whether this is something you should eliminate for now until you get your financial house in order.

As you move to the Short-Term Savings category, your ultimate goal here should be to save at least a couple months' take-home pay. You may need to reduce a selected expense category to achieve your goal more quickly.

The Long-Term Savings category assumes that you work for an employer who puts at least 3 percent of your gross salary into a retirement plan and that you will match it. We will deal with savings and other aspects of your plan in other chapters.

Your spending plan should not be viewed as a downward spiral of deprivation. It is extremely important to build in recreation and fun. We should not spend all of our efforts trying to make sure we have a good life only in the future. While we need to be wise today, tomorrow is not promised to anybody.

It is going to be a lot harder to monitor your ongoing expenditures if you don't have an effective system for doing so. And I can almost guarantee that anyone who doesn't maintain a checking account, but rather cashes his check and pays his bills in cash, will always be financially challenged (read "broke").

Some user-friendly software programs on the market will not only facilitate the writing of checks, but will also make tracking your finances a cinch. At the push of a button, these programs will give you a complete report of income and expenditures by category. Software such as Quicken is available at most computer and office supply stores. These programs also allow you to set up your spending plan and track your actual expenditures against it.

Of course, if you are not computer literate and you want a super simple plan for tracking your expenses, put your budgeted amount of cash for each category in letter-size envelopes for the entire pay period. For example, if "Eating Out" is budgeted at $25, put the $25 in the envelope. When it's gone, no more eating out. Or you may choose to borrow from another category envelope and sacrifice accordingly.

Now that you have prepared your plan, it's time to work it.

> A man's heart plans his way,
>   But the LORD directs his steps.
>   (PROVERBS 16:9)

The plan you set will determine the quality of your life both now and in the future.

7

SECURE YOUR SHORT-TERM AND LONG-TERM FUTURE

People often ask me, "What is the most important thing I can do get my financial house in order?" Actually, you should take a number of important steps to get your financial house in order. Here are some recommendations.

Establish an Emergency Cash Fund

After the 1994 earthquake in Los Angeles, I worked as a special consultant for an entity that provided emergency loans to people who had sustained losses. I was amazed to see how little cash middle-class baby boomers had saved. Many owned homes, cars, and pricey toys that carried huge corresponding loans. Very few had made any preparations for a disaster; cash reserves were virtually nonexistent. Their lifestyle as the "now" generation was very evident. I was reminded of King Solomon's warning,

A prudent person foresees danger and takes precautions.

The simpleton goes blindly on and suffers the consequences.

(PROVERBS 22:3 NLT)

Everybody needs an emergency cash reserve. The amount of the reserve depends on your living expenses. Most financial advisors recommend at least six months, but let's get real. If it costs you $2,000 per month to live, I doubt you will save $12,000 over a short period of time. If you were that disciplined at stashing money away, you probably wouldn't be reading this book. You would have saved and paid cash for the things you charged.

Your ultimate goal should be to accumulate a minimum of two-months' cash reserve at some point in time—but not right now. It may be wiser at this point to have only a month's living expenses in reserve. If you keep your credit card balances low or even designate a special credit card for emergencies only, when something unexpected arises, you can use this card to charge needed items. This is not the same as drawing down a cash advance, which I strongly discourage as the interest rates are usually several points higher than the already exorbitant rate on the regular credit card balance.

Okay, I'm begging you to hear me on this. The U.S. savings rate is now less than 0 percent, which means we are spending more than we make. Save some money! If the one-month cash reserve seems too burdensome, how about having a single paycheck in reserve? $500? $1,000? Start somewhere. You can do it.

Keep Funding Your Retirement

If your employer offers a matching contribution to a retirement account, I am going to assume that you already participate at the maximum level. It is the best investment you can make. For example, say you gross $3,000 per month and your company offers a matching contribution up to 3 percent. This means that for every dollar you put in up to $90, the company will match it. If you contribute $90, you now have $180 per month going toward your retirement. That's an immediate 100 percent return! If you contribute regularly for a number of years, you will have a handsome amount of money when you retire.

If your company does not have a matching contribution plan, then you will want to set up an Individual Retirement Account (IRA). Certain rules and restrictions apply, so you should get more information on this to see if you qualify.

Save Beyond Your Emergency Reserve

Set up a plan whereby you save something each pay period. The most critical aspect of a savings plan is that it be consistent. Try to get an automatic deposit to a savings account. Putting the money in a certificate of deposit or other not-so-easy-to-get-to instrument rather than in a checking account or under your mattress is a great deterrent to frittering those funds away.

Stay on Course with Your Financial Road Map

The first priority for your financial road map is to establish a small emergency cash reserve. Then contribute the maximum amount you can to your company's matching retirement plan, pay down your consumer credit, accumulate a two- to six-months' living expense reserve, and invest in a home, rental property, or other long-term instrument.

Stay balanced in your approach to savings. Learn a lesson from the ants.

> Ants are creatures of little strength,
> yet they store up their food in the summer.
> (PROVERBS 30:25 NIV)

Ants are wise in their forethought and planning. However, we are not to conclude that they save all the food they find in the summer in anticipation of winter. They do eat some of it, otherwise they would perish. And so should it be with us. I have heard couples complain that a spouse just wants to save all of their money for the future with vacations being out of the question. This can cause a marriage to perish.

Speaking of vacations, what about that dream trip? Have you called the travel agency to find out what it will cost and how much you will need to put aside each month to accumulate the necessary amount? Or do you plan to charge the whole thing and spend the next few years paying for it? To accomplish any financial goal, you must have a strategic plan. Just make sure the plan doesn't destroy the quality of your life.

Darnell and I have a general philosophy regarding how we handle our money: give some, save some, spend some.

Maintain Your Insurance

Perhaps you've heard someone remark, "Buying insurance is not biblical. After all, Jesus told His disciples not to worry about tomorrow." Well, let's take a good look at His statement.

> Then He said to His disciples, "Therefore I say to you, do not worry about your life, what you will eat; nor

about the body, what you will put on. Life is more than food, and the body is more than clothing. Consider the ravens, for they neither sow nor reap, which have neither storehouse nor barn; and God feeds them. Of how much more value are you than the birds? And which of you by worrying can add one cubit to his stature? If you then are not able to do the least, why are you anxious for the rest?" (Luke 12:22-26).

Jesus was cautioning His followers not to be anxious about the basic necessities of life—food and clothes. He was not giving them a license to practice poor stewardship over what their heavenly Father had entrusted to them. He was assuring them that if God created them, He was obligated to care for them. God knows that things will happen that are outside of our control. He also knows we can minimize our losses by insuring against them where possible. Let's look at some areas of insurance where we, as good stewards, should focus or refocus our attention.

Medical Insurance. Most people who file for bankruptcy or end up in dire financial straits do so because of uncovered medical expenses. Do everything within your power to obtain or maintain medical coverage. If you are laid off, the company must give you the option of continuing group health benefits at the group rate pursuant to the Consolidated Omnibus Budget Reconciliation Act (COBRA) of 1986. Such coverage is less expensive than what you'd pay if you obtained individual health coverage. The law applies to private-sector employers with 20 or more employees, employee organizations, or state or local governments. You can generally be covered for 18 months. See your employer's health plan administrator for more details.

It is generally unnecessary to obtain insurance coverage for specific medical conditions, such as cancer. Unless the insurance company is going to give you a full rebate of your premium if you have a checkup each year, it's best to insure your whole body and call it a day.

Life Insurance. You can buy two basic types of life insurance: whole-life and term. If you have a whole-life policy, it is not the wonderful investment the insurance salesman told you it was. The company takes your premiums, buys a certain amount of insurance coverage, and invests the difference in some low-return investment. After several years, the investment builds up to a "cash value," and you can borrow against it or cancel the policy and take it directly.

During the early years of the policy, a huge portion of your premiums goes to the salesman as a commission. The plus side of whole-life insurance is that you are covered for your whole life, even when you reach the point where you do not need insurance, such as when you have no more dependents and you have enough money in the bank to pay for your funeral. The premiums on whole-life insurance are a lot higher than those for the same coverage on a term policy. In fact, you could get even more coverage on a term policy for the same amount of money you would pay for a whole-life policy.

But hold on a minute. If you are 50 or older, or if you smoke or have a serious preexisting medical condition, don't run out and cancel your whole-life policy. You may not be able to find a company to write you a term policy.

One lady who heard me teach this in a seminar made an irate call to her whole-life agent for not explaining the benefits of term-life insurance. She was ready to dump the policy without securing the term coverage first.

Do your homework and call several life insurance companies and find out their rates for a term policy. And remember that these policies only cover a certain length of time, such as five to thirty years. Buy coverage for the length of time that fits your need or desire. For example, if you are single and have a 15-year-old, you may want to make sure that if you were to die in the next ten years, you would leave him enough to cover his expenses until he is 25. After that, you may decide he should fend for himself. Therefore, you would buy a 10-year policy. If you die after the term of the policy, too bad! No coverage.

If you are single without a care in the world and no relatives that you feel obligated to bless or support after your death, you need only enough coverage for your burial expenses. Your job probably offers that for free. Why would you go and get a $300,000 policy, even if it is term insurance?

Auto Insurance. If you live in a state where insurance is mandated by law, then get coverage. God requires us to "submit to the government and its officers" (Titus 3:1 NLT). Auto insurance will protect you, so don't skirt it. Do a lot of comparison shopping, calling companies known to offer low rates. A good way to lower your premium is to go for a higher deductible.

If you simply cannot afford the insurance, ask God to provide; He has resources beyond your paycheck or other expected income. Just ask Peter. Jesus instructed him to go fishing to find a coin in a fish's mouth to pay the exact amount of their tax assessment (Matthew 17:24-27).

Mortgage and Other Credit Insurance. If you bought a home, a car, an appliance, or any other major asset, you may have decided to buy credit insurance so that if something happened to you, the outstanding balance would be paid off. This type of insurance is strictly voluntary and is more costly than just buying a general term-life policy that gives your heirs the option of paying off whatever they desire. They may decide it's not in their best interest to pay off certain assets, but rather to do something else with the money.

My advice is to see if you can get out of the policy. But if it makes you sleep better at night knowing that your dependants have this extra coverage, and you have a preexisting medical condition and can't get term insurance, then, as they say in the military, "As you were."

Buying appropriate insurance is good stewardship. We know God has us covered for every circumstance, but He has given us the sense and the responsibility to anticipate potential losses and to take precautions.

8

MASTER YOUR DEBTS

D ebt is the slave master of the masses. We are a nation of consumers who have used credit to instantly gratify our desires and medicate our insecurities. Recent surveys revealed that the average American family spends approximately 125 percent of its gross income and maintains average credit card balances of $9,400. Excess consumer debt is evidence that we are spending money we *wish* we earned. Someone once said, "The trouble with most people is their earning capacity doesn't match their yearning capacity."

God's position on debt is very clear; it puts the borrower in bondage to the lender.

> The rich rules over the poor,
>> And the borrower is servant to the lender.
>>> (PROVERBS 22:7)

When you can make only the minimum payments on your credit cards for months at a time, you are in bondage. When you can't even begin to dream about a real vacation because of your debt, you are in bondage. When you can never make a gift to special projects at your church because of your debt, you are in bondage. Many churches have to go into debt to finance building projects because their members are in debt. If everyone were debt free and embraced the principles of tithes and offerings, churches would not need to borrow.

While the Scriptures do not prohibit us from incurring debt, in each instance where debt is discussed, negativity surrounds it. Because debt limits our freedom to make choices about the rest of our life, it would seem wise to minimize or eliminate it. Our ultimate goal should be to become debt free.

Good Debt vs. Bad Debt

Not all debt is bad. A residential mortgage has historically been good debt. When you purchase a home, you invest in an asset that will usually increase in value over the long haul, stabilize your housing costs, provide a tax write-off, give you credibility, and become a significant factor in your retirement planning. However, a mortgage that is beyond your ability to pay is a bad debt that brings all kinds of other woes and vastly reduces the quality of your life. If, as a rule of thumb, you target your mortgage payment to be no more than 25-28 percent of your income, you'd have a better shot at balancing your life and providing for retirement. The percentage may increase in states where property values are higher; but in those situations, it would still be wise to limit it to no more than 33 percent of your income.

A college loan is another example of good debt. By getting an education, you increase your ability to make a good income. That's why the people who extended you the loan won't let you off the hook—even if you file bankruptcy.

The amount you owe on your department store credit card is bad debt. If you analyze the items you purchased, they represent things you desired rather than things you needed. In some cases, the balances on your cards include items you consumed years ago.

Auto loans are not necessarily bad, for you may need transportation to your job. But if you purchase a status car that is beyond your budget, then you have entered the realm of bad debt. Let's get real. A car, unless it is a classic, is not an investment. Investments should increase in value; the value of a car decreases when you drive it off the dealer's lot.

Credit Card Debt

Having a fistful of credit cards was once impressive, but now it is irresponsible. Normally you need to maintain only one card for additional identification or if you travel, rent cars, or stay in hotels. However, during a national credit crisis, owning two or even three credit cards may be a wiser choice as credit limits may be cut on each one. If you have only one card, then your access to credit may be severely limited when your credit ceiling is lowered. MasterCard and Visa are more widely accepted than others, so they are the cards I recommend.

You must learn to be smart in using your credit cards. It would be wise to use credit cards that offer travel miles or other perks. Make the cards work for you. Use "their" money interest free by paying all bills in full when they arrive.

If you can't pay in full, at least make your minimum payment as soon as the bill arrives. Don't allow the bill to sit around waiting for the due date and collecting interest when you have adequate funds to make the payment. The sooner the bank gets your check, the less interest you pay. Do whatever is necessary to avoid delinquencies.

Understand the terms of your credit card agreement. Over 40 percent of credit cards carry a "universal default" clause. The interest rate on your credit card may be increased if you pay a bill more than 30 days late to *another* creditor, even if you pay your credit card bill on time. This is outrageous, but there is no law against it. I have heard horror stories of people being slapped with huge rate increases on their credit cards just because they paid a phone bill late. The universal default clause is usually explained in the fine print, so get out your latest credit card billing and read every word on the back and front. Call the company and ask for an explanation of anything you do not understand. Don't worry about taking up their time; they can afford lots of staff to answer your questions.

A good understanding of the real cost of using a credit card may be enough to cause you to resort to "plastic surgery." If you were to make only the minimum payment each month on your credit card bill with a $5,000 balance, for example, it would take more than 26 years at an interest cost of over $7,000 to pay it off.

Understanding how disadvantaged you are by paying only the minimum payment is really quite simple. First, divide the minimum payment by the outstanding balance. This tells you what percentage of the balance the payment represents. Let's assume that your outstanding balance is $2,500 and the minimum required payment is $62.50. This represents 2.5 percent of the outstanding balance ($62.50/$2,500). Next, note your annual interest rate as indicated on the front of your statement. Assume 18 percent for this example. Divide it by 12 to compute your monthly interest rate; this comes to 1.5 percent (the interest portion of your monthly payment). Now here is the part that you need to be savvy about. Note that your minimum payment is 2.5 percent and your interest is 1.5 percent which is included in the minimum payment; the difference is the amount that your balance will be reduced by, i.e., 1 percent (2.5 percent minimum payment minus 1.5 percent monthly interest). That's not very much. Finally, using this example, of the $62.50 minimum payment, only 1 percent ($25) of the $2,500 outstanding balance this month will go to reduce the balance. The rest of the minimum payment ($37.50) will go to interest. Pretty pricey, huh?

If you are a good paying customer, you need to call up the credit card company and ask them to reduce your interest rate or you'll consider a company who has lower rates. Go ahead; try it on all your cards.

Before you plop down that plastic, ask yourself, "If I had to go to the bank and apply for a loan to pay for this, would I buy it?" Well, credit cards are nothing more than preapproved, high-interest bank loans. If you charge anything and cannot pay it in full when the bill comes, consider yourself in trouble—unless you are deliberately trying to build a credit history by showing that you can make monthly payments. Even so, keep the funds in reserve to pay the amount in full.

Consolidating your debt into one payment may sound like a bright idea, especially if you obtain a home equity loan to do so. You will pay a lot less interest on a home equity loan than you would on each credit card. Plus, the interest becomes tax deductible up to a certain limit. However, you now have a greater potential for getting into even more debt because you have paid off those credit card balances. If you don't cut the cards up or hand them over to a trusted friend, you could find yourself in an even deeper hole, and now your house is on the line.

Fast Tracking Out of Debt

Let's look at a simple plan for digging out of debt. Start with the debt that has the lowest balance. This is the one you will pay off first because that will free up cash sooner to apply to remaining debts. You will feel a sense of accomplishment once a single debt has been eliminated, and you will have greater incentive to keep up the good work. (You would actually save more money over the long run by first paying off the debt with the highest interest rate, but most credit card holders develop "payment fatigue" and start to slack off after two or three years.) Add an extra amount (the more the better) to the minimum monthly payment of the card you targeted for payoff. Where do you find the "extra amount"? Try taking your lunch and snacks to work three days a week. This may yield an extra $50 per month. And do you really need all of those extra telephone services or television cable boxes?

Continue paying the minimum payment on all other debts until the smallest debt is paid off. When this debt is paid in full, take the amount (the minimum plus the extra payment you have been paying) and add it to the minimum payment on debt number two.

If you faithfully follow this strategy, you will turbocharge your way out of debt in remarkable time. Decide now what you will do with the money once all of the debt is paid off. This is not the time to celebrate with a spending spree. Try finding another way to reward yourself.

Once you have paid down your cards, it's important not to put yourself in a position where you will be tempted to incur additional debt. The apostle Paul warned, "Make no provision for the flesh, to fulfill its lusts" (Romans 13:14). If you still frequent the mall, even for an occasional walk, you are making provision to fulfill your shopping desire. It's like putting mice in charge of the cheese. To minimize your risk, take only enough money to the mall to buy the necessity that caused you to go there.

Make every effort to get and stay out of debt. You can't begin to plan for investments that may yield a 5 to 15 percent return when you are burdened with debt costing you 18 to 22 percent. Do the math. Transfer the discipline that you exercise in other areas of your life to mastering your debts.

Your FICO Score

Being credit savvy is critical especially as it relates to your FICO score. As explained in chapter 1, the score goes up to 850. You will find yourself at a real disadvantage if your score is under 675. The higher your score, the lower your interest rate will be on your debt.

The two most significant factors affecting your score are your bill-paying history and the outstanding balances on your credit cards when compared to the credit limits on these cards. For example, if you owe $8,000 on all of your consumer debt and have a limit of $10,000, then you are 80 percent maxed out. This is not viewed favorably. However, if you have a total limit of $32,000 on all your cards and you owe $8,000, then you owe only 25 percent of what you could owe. Now this shows that you have exercised some discipline. That's why you must be careful not to immediately run out and cancel your cards because you will lower your total available credit limit.

Your goal should be to achieve a FICO score of at least 700. How do you do this? First, check your credit report to make sure there isn't an error on it that is dragging down your score. Most credit reports will have some sort of inaccuracy. Second, pay your bills on time. Third, pay off as many bills as you can so that you can reduce the percentage of your total credit limit that is outstanding.

Think strategically. Keep the credit cards you've had a long time (you need the history on your record) and just cut up a few excess ones. The FICO spy won't know that you cut them up; he'll just think that you are exercising discipline by not using them.

When You Are Overwhelmed with Debt

You may feel isolated and overwhelmed in your attempt to get your finances under control. Don't try to solve your problems alone. From friends to formal debt-counseling agencies, help is only a call away. As the Book of Proverbs reminds us,

> Plans go wrong for lack of advice;
> many advisers bring success.
> (PROVERBS 15:22 NLT)

The first place to seek help when your finances are out of control is from a trusted, financially astute, Bible-believing friend or family member who can give you caring support, good advice, and help you to stay accountable. "Carry each other's burdens, and in this way you will fulfill the law of Christ" (Galatians 6:2 NIV).

However, I find that most people are too embarrassed to let

someone know about the bad judgment that got them to where they are. This kind of thinking will keep you in the red. Ask the Holy Spirit to help you get beyond the shame so that you can quickly make your escape from financial bondage. If it is of any comfort, tons of people are in your same situation.

A few years ago I sat down with a close relative who was in dire financial straits. We spent hours poring over credit card bills, payroll check stubs, and other documents. She had gone through a divorce, and her husband had been irresponsible in handling his finances. A car repossession, various delinquency charges, and a few other financial dings painted a bleak picture for her future credit. Further, to ease the emotional impact of the divorce and to get back into the swing of things, she had resorted to "mall therapy" and had run up quite a few credit card bills.

While I was sympathetic to her plight, even wanting to bail her out by consolidating all of her consumer debt into a personal loan, I decided she needed the discipline of digging her way out of the hole. I cringed even more when I saw that she hardly gave anything to her church. Although I didn't see a way that she could do it, I still suggested that she begin to give God His due.

We worked out a strategic plan that she committed to follow, and I made some accountability calls over the next few months. Three years later, she now pays her tithes and is on stable financial footing. She also purchased a home and has been promoted several times on her job.

If you do not have a relative or friend who can provide guidance and accountability, and you really don't have a clue what to do, you may want to try a credit counseling agency. Over nine million debt-challenged Americans seek help from credit-counseling agencies annually.

In recent years, some agencies have received a bad reputation for pressuring clients to pay high "voluntary" fees and for quickly putting them into debt-management plans that require high fees. There have been a few horror stories of debt-management firms collecting funds for clients' monthly bills and not sending timely payments to the creditors. Therefore, it would be wise to make every effort to find a reputable Christian agency whose advice is based upon biblical principles and that takes time to understand your circumstances.

Be sure the agency puts in writing the fees they will charge and that you understand and can afford them. Absent a personal referral, do an Internet search to find one in your area. Stay away from secular agencies that may encourage you to put your obligation to God on the back burner until it makes more sense on paper. You are going to need favor and supernatural intervention to get your finances back on track. Giving shows that you are exercising your faith and planting seeds for the power of God to work in your life. "But my righteous one will live by faith. And if he shrinks back, I will not be pleased with him" (Hebrews 10:38 NIV).

Here's the bottom line on what you can expect from a credit-counseling agency:

- They will charge you a setup fee and a monthly maintenance fee for their services.
- They will contact your creditors to work out lower payments, request a stop to late fees and other penalties, and even work out a reduction or elimination of interest charges.
- They do not contact utilities, insurance companies, or secured creditors (those who hold a security interest

in the things you have purchased, such as your home and cars).

If this is the kind of help you need to get out of the red, go for it.

> Listen to advice and accept instruction,
> and in the end you will be wise.
> (PROVERBS 19:20)

If the thought of potential credit-counseling fraud scares you away, you may decide to go solo in working your way out of the pit. Do not despair. You know what to do. Develop a plan and work it. Be patient. It took more than a month to get where you are, and it will take more than a month to get out of the red. It really is like dieting. Just be consistent in applying the principles we've discussed.

Strategies When Facing a Foreclosure

If you find yourself facing the possibility of losing your home through a foreclosure, consider the strategies below to help you get through and even embrace this challenge. Even if you are not facing such a predicament, being educated about the process will empower you to help others.

Leasing Out Your Home

Before you become delinquent on your mortgage payments, you might want to lease your home out and move to less expensive quarters. This is a viable option if the income from the lease will cover the mortgage, property taxes, and other expenses on your home, or if you have the ability to subsidize a portion of those payments if the lease income does not cover them in full. It's also worth the expense to use a landlord services company to at least screen the lease applicants. Be very careful. Some potential tenants are professional squatters who come out of the woodwork during times of economic upheaval.

I talked to a friend recently who could no longer make her mortgage payments. She told me a horror story of leasing her beautiful home in a posh neighborhood to a woman who pulled every trick in the book to avoid paying the rent and had cost my friend tens of thousands of dollars in unnecessary repairs and legal and other expenses. Tenants referred to you by trusted friends are usually a better choice.

Working with Your Lender

If leasing out your home is not an option, here are some strategies to help you get through the crisis.

Communicate with Your Lender. As soon as you see the handwriting on the wall or have an inkling of trouble with paying your mortgage, don't go into denial or hiding. Contact your lender's loss mitigation department—not the collections department, which typically offers one option: Pay now! Explain your circumstances and be honest about the maximum amount you can pay. Make a specific request for a reduction in your monthly payment amount and back it up with documentation of your current income and expenses.

Request a Temporary Fix When Appropriate. If your delinquency is due to a temporary situation and you see the light at the end of the tunnel, consider these options:

- *Forbearance.* Your mortgage payments may be reduced or delayed for a specific number of months. You will officially agree to a payment schedule for catching up the past due amounts.

- *Reinstatement.* If you know for sure that you can bring the account current by a set date by paying a lump sum, the lender may allow you to do so.
- *Repayment plan.* If you have the cash flow to resume your regular payments but are not able to pay all of the delinquent amounts, some lenders will allow you to add an extra amount to your regular payments until you are caught up.

If you see no way to pursue any of these three options, you might need to go down a different path.

Refinance the Loan. This is called a *mortgage modification.* The lender could agree to combine the past due interest and the current loan balance into a new mortgage at a new interest rate and a longer term, resulting in lower payments. Rather than the traditional 30-year mortgage, some lenders offer 40- and 50-year terms. There's a good chance the mortgage will outlive you! Do I need to remind you that the longer a debt is outstanding the more interest you'll pay? Consider this when evaluating your decision.

Throw in the Towel. No, this is not defeatist thinking; you just have to know when it's best to let go to relieve the financial and emotional load of holding on to a house that you can no longer afford. Once you make the decision, you will probably experience immediate relief. Throwing in the towel may take the following forms:

- *Pre-foreclosure sale.* The lender may allow you a period of time to sell the house at a price that will pay off the loan in full.
- *Deed in lieu of foreclosure.* This option allows you to

voluntarily transfer ownership of your property to your lender without going through the foreclosure process. They simply "call it even." Most lenders will require you to use your best efforts to sell the property first. The impact on your credit, though negative, will be less significant.

• *Short sale.* If you owe significantly more on your house than its current market value, the lender may allow you to sell it at a substantial discount and accept the proceeds as payment in full. For example, if you owe $300,000 on your home and it's worth only $200,000, the lender may accept that as payment in full.

In the past, many lenders would go after the borrower for the difference, though most would forgive the shortfall amount and report it as income to the IRS, creating additional taxable income for the borrower. Historically, the Internal Revenue Service has considered forgiven debt as taxable income. However, the Mortgage Forgiveness Debt Relief Act of 2007 waived the federal income taxes for short sales and deeds-in-lieu of foreclosures occurring from January 1, 2007 to December 31, 2009.

Except for the pre-foreclosure sale and leasing suggestions, all of the options discussed above will negatively affect your credit. Therefore, you must choose the one that is best for your situation and get the issue behind you. This too will pass, and soon you'll be on the road to rebuilding your good credit.

Other Strategies

As a final caution, beware of scams when facing a foreclosure. Unscrupulous real estate or loan professionals are lurking in the dark waiting to victimize you. I had a relative who was in foreclosure when a local firm offered to conduct all the negotiations with her lender for a $2,500 fully refundable fee if they were unsuccessful in restructuring the loan. She informed them of the status of the loan when she filled out the application for their services, so they knew that the situation was beyond their influence when they accepted her funds. Still, they promised results. When they were unsuccessful in getting any concessions, they balked at returning her funds. I made several calls on her behalf, threatened to take the case to the highest level possible, and finally persuaded them to refund her fee.

(To educate you on scam artists, Freddie Mac has posted a video titled "Foreclosure Scams 101." Check it out at www.you tube.com/AvoidFraud [last accessed October 2008]).

Beware of unscrupulous lenders who offer high-risk second mortgages. You just may be postponing the inevitable. Have a knowledgeable person review the terms. Don't be intimidated by the lender's aggressiveness. Only sign what you understand.

Whatever you do, if you hope to get any assistance, do not move out of your home unless you have been given a notice to vacate. In order to qualify for assistance, homeowners are often required to be living in their home. So be sure to talk to your lender before you think about moving.

Operate in integrity to the very end. Do not destroy or deface the property. Yes, you may be hurt and angry over your unfortunate circumstances, but don't miss the life lessons you could be learning that will protect you in the future.

Besides, you will reap what you sow. Why sow negative seeds?

9

SOW SEEDS OF GENEROSITY

In times of economic uncertainty, it's tempting to slack off in giving to the church or in helping others. Many people put the work of God on the back burner with the intention of resuming their giving once the financial crisis is over. But the essence of a God-honoring financial plan is to determine the best way, as a steward or manager, to handle *God's* money that He has entrusted to you. The real issue is not how much of *your* money you plan to give to God, but rather how much of *His* money you will keep for yourself.

Tithes

The top priority in a God-honoring financial strategy is to address your obligation to Him through paying your tithe. The tithe is the first 10 percent of your income. Many people debate whether tithing is strictly an Old Testament law that became obsolete under the New Covenant. Some have even argued that we cannot use Jesus' words in Matthew 23:23 as justification for tithing today.

"What sorrow awaits you teachers of religious law and you Pharisees. Hypocrites! For you are careful to tithe even the tiniest income from your herb gardens, but you ignore the more important aspects of the law—justice, mercy, and faith. You *should* tithe, yes, but do not neglect the more important things" (Matthew 23:23 NLT, emphasis added).

Now, if Jesus says I should do something, I'm not about to debate the issue.

If you are among those who say you cannot afford to tithe, I want to tell you why this may be so. You may not have made this act of worship the top priority in your finances. The Scriptures admonish,

> *Honor* the LORD with your possessions,
> And with the *first*fruits of all your increase.
> (PROVERBS 3:9)

What you are really saying is that by the time you pay all your bills and other priorities, nothing is left. Well, dear friend, God doesn't want what's left; He wants what's right. You can always afford anything that comes off the top.

I'm convinced that God has been faithful in providing for me because I've been faithful in paying my tithes. In our 30 years of marriage, Darnell and I have never missed paying our tithes. We know this is a miracle in itself since several times it looked as though we needed the money to close the financial gap on a transaction or for other purposes. But we just stayed the course and never stopped taking it off the top.

I view my tithes the same way I view my car insurance premiums. The state of California requires that every vehicle owner purchase insurance. Paying for the coverage is in the best interest of the owner, for it protects him, not against accidents but against *loss*. Because I've obeyed the law and purchased the insurance, I can rest assured that I will not lose everything I own if I have a car accident. In the same way, when I pay my tithe, I am insuring myself, not against incidents and economic conditions, but against *lack*. Because I have fulfilled the requirement, I rest assured that God has me covered financially.

If you are a tither and are still struggling, remember God's challenge to the people of Israel when they were withholding their tithes following their return from captivity:

> "Bring all the tithes into the storehouse so there will
> be enough food in my Temple. If you do," says the
> LORD of Heaven's Armies, "I will open the windows
> of heaven for you. I will pour out a blessing so great
> you won't have enough room to take it in! Try it! Put
> me to the test!" (Malachi 3:10 NLT).

You may be contributing to your financial dilemma by not handling the remaining 90 percent of your income with wisdom and in accordance with biblical principles. Review your current expenditures and see which ones you can reduce or do without for a season. Know that tithing is an act of obedience and faith.

I began paying my tithe when I received $10 per month as an allowance from my dad during my early college years. Today, Darnell and I tithe and also make contributions to special projects and other needs of the church. I am so grateful that my spiritual mentors taught me to tithe early in my life. I believe it is much harder to begin tithing when you make a big salary than when the tithe is small. Satan will always magnify the amount and try to convince you that it's too much money to give away. Whatever income I receive,

I know that at least 10 percent of it belongs to God, and I make no plans to use that portion. Further, for unexpected amounts, I will stop and ask God if there is someone I need to bless. Many times He uses us as a channel for His resources. I heard someone say, "God will get it to you when He knows He can get it through you."

Someone asked me the other day, "How can I tithe when I make no money?" Well, if you make absolutely no money, then you owe no tithes. God gives you the seed that He wants you to sow; if He doesn't give you any seed, He doesn't require any sowing. "Now may He who supplies seed to the sower, and bread for food, supply and multiply the seed you have sown and increase the fruits of your righteousness" (2 Corinthians 9:10).

Offerings

Notice that we pay the tithe (or tenth) because it is required. A second level of giving over and above the tithe is offerings. An offering is like the tip on a meal in a restaurant. To say, "I'm just going to give an offering because I can't tithe" is like saying, "I'm just going to give a tip because I cannot afford to pay for the food." Along with our tithes, God expects offerings, evidenced by His question in Malachi 3:8: " 'Will a man rob God? Yet you rob me. But you ask, "How do we rob you?" In tithes *and offerings*' " (emphasis added). The amount you give for your offering and to whom you give it is entirely up to you.

Alms

The third level of financial obedience is alms or charity. These are the deeds we do for others in the form of money or goods. Some people think they can distribute some of their tithes directly to the poor in the form of alms. Know that we are required to bring all of the tithes to God's house for its provisions. If you attend a church that does not help the needy, consider whether or not it's the place God has called you to worship. Don't just decide that you will fix the problem by redirecting your tithes.

God places great value on alms. Proverbs 19:17 says,

> He who has pity on the poor lends to the LORD,
> And He will pay back what he has given.

Imagine it. When you help someone in need, God in essence writes out an IOU. And He never forgets it. He just keeps paying you back again and again. Look at what He did for the widow who shared the very last of her food with the prophet Elijah. When he asked her to bring him some bread, she informed him that she and her son did not have enough to meet even their own need. Nevertheless, "She did as Elijah said, and she and Elijah and her son continued to eat for many days. There was always enough flour and olive oil left in the containers, just as the Lord had promised through Elijah" (1 Kings 17:15-16 NLT).

God rewards obedience.

Cornelius, the New Testament centurion, also gave generously to those in need. When God decided to bless him and his household by sending Peter to him with the gospel, He sent him this message by an angel: "Your prayers and gifts to the poor have come up as a memorial offering before God" (Acts 10:4 NIV). A memorial keeps something in perpetual memory. Cornelius simply helped the poor, and God chose to reward him.

Many years ago, my husband and I sent a very worn and worthy evangelist on a trip that we ourselves had long desired to take. Knowing she needed the rest and the serenity of that luxurious Hawaiian island, and also realizing she could not afford such a treat, we willingly sponsored the trip for her and her husband. Since then, we have reaped—and continue to reap—many wonderful trips from that seed. From luxury cruises at low or no cost to first-class excursions to the uttermost parts of the world, the Lord has demonstrated His faithfulness. I never fail to remember that each trip has been a result of that alms-giving seed.

If you want to make a difference in your finances, trust God and begin to pay your tithes, give offerings, and help the poor. You really can't beat God at giving.

Learn to Receive

Receiving is the flip side of the giving coin. While you may not give to get, it is biblical to give and to expect God to honor His Word to those who give. However, it's hard to receive some things if you don't ask for them. Asking can sometimes be scary—especially if the thing you request is for a benefit or a concession that is not normally granted. Even if most people attempt to ask, they will usually retreat at the first hint of resistance. The worst that could happen is that someone will say no—in which case you are right back where you started. If you are going to survive and thrive during economic uncertainty, you will eventually need favor from somebody. Favor can bring you to a place that money cannot.

Asking for favor is a biblical principle that most of us are reluctant to apply. God often gives us favor without our having to ask for it. However, there are times when some things will not come to fruition until we make our request known.

The story of the five daughters of Zelophehad (Numbers 27:1-11) is a great example of how it pays to ask for what you want. Because their father had died in the wilderness and they had no brothers, they asked Moses to grant them their father's portion of the property in the Promised Land. At that time, only men could inherit land. God gave Moses the okay, and He not only granted their request, but also changed the law for future generations of women who would find themselves in similar circumstances. You must not assume that anyone is going to have as great a concern for your finances as you do. You must be proactive in getting what you want.

Jesus encouraged His disciples to be persistent in prayer by giving them an example of a man who had unexpected guests arrive and no bread to give them. He went to his friend's house late at night and asked for three loaves. Since the friend and his family were already in bed, the friend told him to come back tomorrow. However, the man was not to be deterred. He kept asking until he wearied his friend. Jesus concluded the parable by giving the moral of the story: "I say to you, though he will not rise and give to him because he is his friend, yet because of his persistence he will rise and give him as many as he needs" (Luke 11:8).

Why are some people reluctant to ask for favor? Do they think others will resent them if they get an unfair advantage? Are they afraid that the person they are asking will no longer like them or will see them as a troublemaker? Do they fear being perceived as someone who does not want to work or pay for every single thing they obtain? Is their self-esteem so low that they think they don't deserve favorable treatment from anyone? Are they such control freaks that they feel a favor will put them in debt to someone?

I'm amused by people who always want to be on the giving end but cannot receive from others. When I had this mind-set, I realized that subconsciously I liked having people feel as though they owed me something. It kept them in relational debt to me. If they repaid me by giving me something back, that made us even, and I no longer held the advantage in the relationship. This way of thinking is very subtle and often denied, but when you let God shine the light on your heart, you can be healed of your controlling ways and will find it easier to receive from others.

I make every effort to plant the seeds of favor in whatever way I can. I have often provided financial consulting for free or at discounted rates for those who could not afford it—or even those who could. Further, I share information and professional contacts with people who would be considered competitors. I have also learned not to protest when I receive favor in return. I simply acknowledge it as a manifestation of the Word of God: "Give, and it will be given to you: good measure, pressed down, shaken together, and running over will be put into your bosom" (Luke 6:38).

When I was awarded a fellowship to pursue a postgraduate degree, I asked the private foundation that had granted my undergraduate student loan to defer payments until I graduated. They agreed and waived additional interest charges to boot. Favor, favor.

Is there a financial favor you need to ask for today? Do you need someone to reduce an outstanding debt? To extend a loan for your business? To give you a concession on car repairs? To defer payments without it showing up on your credit? To babysit your children at a minimal cost?

Well, are you righteous—that is, in right standing with your heavenly Father? If so, then expect favor. You're surrounded with it!

> For surely, O LORD, you bless the righteous;
>   you surround them with your favor as with a
>   shield.

(PSALM 5:12)

Be bold and expect a yes! Caution. When *no* is the final answer to your persistence, submit your desires to God's sovereign plan. He is working out something better. Stay sensitive to His Spirit, and remember that no one can thwart God's purpose for your life (Isaiah 14:27).

10

SPEND WISELY

We need the wisdom of God in our spending as never before. Darnell and I have made more than our fair share of spontaneous investments in nonappreciating items that we later regretted. We have now learned to ponder our purchases. Let me share a few of these experiences so you can learn from our mistakes.

Some Guidelines for Wise Spending

Stop Impulse Buying

"We'll take it!" we told the car salesman. When we left home that nice breezy morning, Darnell and I had no intention of returning with a brand-new red convertible. We had driven to a certain area to take a walk, and on the way home decided to stop by an auto dealership to indulge our curiosity. We were not even driving the car we would have traded in for this nice little upgrade. Several hours later, after the standard routine of the salesman checking with the manager in the back office a dozen times to get approval on the price, we drove off into the sunset.

The next day, reality set in as we realized we would need to sell our old car right away as well as pay for insurance on three vehicles. When all was said and done, the monthly cost of this car would equal the mortgage payment on an investment property in a good working-class neighborhood. We sold the car several months later and bought the property.

The Scriptures warn against impulsiveness:

> The plans of the diligent lead to profit
> as surely as haste leads to poverty.
> (PROVERBS 21:5 NIV)

This tendency toward haste is what leads us down the path to debt. We are the "now" generation, and we do not like to delay our gratification.

Many times God tries to protect us from our hasty decisions by throwing up red flags and putting up roadblocks. But what do we often do? Put our heads in the sand and ignore them. Be careful if you're about to enter a transaction and things start falling apart.

My husband and I once invested in an ATM. (Yes, you read right—a machine that dispenses money.) The company's sales pitch was very enticing. The salesman, who claimed he was a Christian, convinced us that investing in an ATM was the ideal way to make our money "work for us" with no effort on our part except to lease the machine for five years and own it at the end of that time. He promised—not in writing (red flag...red flag...red flag!)—that he would find the ideal location, put up appropriate signs, and the whole nine yards.

After we signed the lease agreement, he came back and said he had computed the payment incorrectly and that it would be an extra $50 per month (red flag...red flag...red flag!). Well, he reneged on all of his promises, and his company accepted no responsibility for them. He skipped town and left us with a non-cancelable $426 monthly lease payment while the machine sat in our garage. We never found a profitable location for it and ended up selling it at a substantial loss several years later.

How did we fall into this trap? First, we were too busy to pay attention to the details. Second, we assumed that the salesperson was sincere about his Christian faith. We are now extremely cautious of investing in a deal solely because the promoter comes "in the name of Jesus." Finally, we didn't want to be like the wicked, lazy steward Jesus spoke of in Matthew 25 who buried rather than invested the money he had been entrusted with. We really were trying to be good stewards. We wanted to maximize the return on our idle funds. We are much smarter today.

Now back to haste. When you recall the things you have bought on a whim, they were rarely items you needed. Rather, they represented temporary, emotion-filled desires. Even if you are certain that something is a great idea, you should make it a habit of pondering your purchases.

Beware of hot deals and clearance sales. If you don't need an item and have no plans to use it, then it is not a good deal no matter how low the price. I have tons of stuff I've bought at a steal but have never worn. Impulsiveness makes you good bait for hungry salespeople, dishonest promoters, and other sales ploys.

And speaking of salespeople, don't succumb to high-pressure deadlines. If it's meant for you to purchase an item, it will still be there the next day. Give yourself 24 hours to think about big-ticket purchases. Before you buy, ask yourself,

- "Is this a need or a desire?"
- "Can I afford it?"
- "Will I use it immediately?"
- "Do I already have something similar?"
- "How can I glorify God with this purchase?"

On a smaller scale of impulsiveness, I also challenge you to be on the alert when you're standing in line at the grocery store. Remember that the merchandise at the checkout counter is strategically positioned to encourage you to spend more money. You must prepare to resist the lure of sugar-laden snacks, gossip magazines, movies, and other impulse items.

I have always been intrigued by the financial behavior of the Proverbs 31 superwoman. Her lack of impulsiveness is inspiring. "She considers a field and buys it" (Proverbs 31:16). When you ponder your purchases, the Holy Spirit will often flash the red light of disapproval. Don't run it.

> In all your ways acknowledge Him,
> And He shall direct your paths.
> (PROVERBS 3:6)

Limit Your Luxuries

"Wear the things of this world like loose garments." These were words often spoken by one of my spiritual mentors, the late Dr. Juanita Smith. The essence of her warning was that we should not cling to anything so tightly that we cannot give it up.

How married are you to your current lifestyle? Have you enjoyed certain luxuries for such a long time that you feel entitled to them? The Bible warns us against the pursuit of pleasure:

Those who love pleasure become poor;
   those who love wine and luxury will never be
   rich.
(PROVERBS 21:17 NLT)

If you are trying to control your finances, then it's time to distinguish between your necessities and your luxuries. You may have to forego a luxury or two in order to reach your financial goals. Jesus let go of the luxuries of heaven in order to achieve His goal on earth.

Your attitude should be the same as that of
   Christ Jesus:
Who, being in very nature God,
   did not consider equality with God
      something to be grasped,
but made himself nothing,
   taking the very nature of a servant,
   being made in human likeness.
(PHILIPPIANS 2:5-7 NIV)

"Well, that sounds good in theory, but how do I make it happen?" a certain man asked me.

First of all, it depends on how big of a mess you're in, how ingrained your luxuries are, and how badly you want to get on the road to financial freedom. Second, you must realize that you will need divine enablement to exercise the discipline to let some things go. Jesus reminds us that "apart from me you can do nothing" (John 15:5 NIV). For every step you will take in your journey to your financial goals, you must stop and ask God for the strength to go forward. Here is how one couple got out of the pit:

When we first got married 14 years ago, my wife and I were young and uneducated about finances. We both had credit cards with balances, car payments, and so forth. We had never really added up just how much we owed. Once married, my wife added it all up. Credit cards alone topped $25,000, about half of our pretax combined income. We set out a plan to pay off the debt and buy a house in two years. We cut way back, took no long vacations, and did not set foot in a restaurant for nine months. Others told us our goal was too aggressive, but we did it. Today, we still do not manage our money as well as we should, but we have no credit card debt and we wait until we have the cash to make purchases.

For this couple, long vacations and eating out were luxuries. I won't dictate what pleasures you should consider giving up for a season, but just in case you've fallen in love and married all of your luxuries, here is a list to consider:

- morning lattes from your favorite coffee shop
- the daily paper
- weekly manicures and pedicures
- daily snacks from the catering truck
- biweekly golf outings

Believe it or not, these items add up over time. I'm not saying to eliminate them. I don't think total deprivation is a good thing because it can lead to a binge later. You only need to let go of these nonessentials for a season, or just limit your indulgence in them until your finances are on solid footing.

What a great time to forge new values. Why not aspire to the apostle Paul's testimony? "I know how to live on almost nothing or with everything. I have learned the secret of living in every situation, whether it is with a full stomach or empty, with plenty or little" (Philippians 4:12 NLT).

Unlike smoking, drinking, and other bad habits you must completely eliminate to escape their clutches and consequences, shopping is necessary to sustain your life. Therefore, the key to keeping it from becoming a vice is to exercise wisdom and discipline in how you spend. Let's look at some common areas where you can be a smart shopper.

Resist TV Shopping Channels

Infomercials have seduced many into buying items that they don't need or use once they've acquired them. Don't be fooled by the convenience of ordering these items with their money-back guarantees and their 30 percent shipping and handling charges, which are never refundable. Only recently have I overcome my weakness for exercise gear and miracle diet products or any other "breakthrough" merchandise touted on infomercials for three easy payments of $19.99 per month. The last straw was when I purchased a set of pots and pans guaranteed to outperform stainless steel. I never took the plastic wrapping off; I finally gave them to Goodwill. I have yet to order anything that performed the way it was advertised. I'm sure there are things out there that work, but I'm throwing in the towel on miracle products.

Buy Pre-Owned Clothes

When God decided to bring the Israelites out of Egyptian bondage, He provided them a quality wardrobe from their oppressors that would sustain them during their wilderness trek. "Every Israelite woman will ask for articles of silver and gold and fine clothing from her Egyptian neighbors and from the foreign women in their houses. You will dress your sons and daughters with these" (Exodus 3:22 NLT). God could have easily dropped new clothes out of the sky whenever necessary. After all, He did so with their daily food supply.

When you're trying to rein in unruly finances, buying brand new may not be the best option. Are you too proud to wear used clothing from thrift or other secondhand stores? I know some pretty high-level folks who pride themselves on the deals they find in such places. Try the ones near exclusive neighborhoods, and you'll be amazed at the quality of the merchandise.

Invest in Basic Clothing

When you must limit your shopping budget, consider buying items that you can pair with other outfits in your wardrobe. Do you really think it's wise to buy those hot pink shoes to match those hot pink pants? Why not try a black pair you can wear over and over again? Before you go shopping, do a quick inventory of your closet to see which basics (white shirt, black skirts, etc.) are most needed. If you must, you can buy some relatively inexpensive trendy accessories to spruce up your wardrobe. Just remember that next season they will probably be outdated.

Buy Used Cars

I have heard many financially challenged Christians testify that, in spite of their poor credit history, God blessed them with a brand-new upscale vehicle from a sympathetic car dealer. What is not stated is that it comes with a large monthly payment that reflects an exorbitant interest rate, or an unusually long repayment schedule that is sure to guarantee the lender a healthy profit. In many cases, the exuberant recipient will have to exercise more faith to meet the payments than he did to get the car in the first place. What looked like a blessing is really a burden in disguise.

I am often reminded that "the blessing of the LORD makes a person rich, and he adds no sorrow with it" (Proverbs 10:22 NLT). Because a new vehicle loses so much of its value when you drive it off the lot, a two- to three-year-old used car is usually a better investment. But before you buy, make sure you have the car checked out by a good mechanic.

Work Special Events

A good way to maintain a great social life at no expense is to volunteer to serve as an usher or to provide other support at various events. Just check out the social section of your newspaper and call the sponsors to see what help is needed. You'll get a chance to hobnob with folks with money. Who knows where that may lead? After all, God gives His children favor with man.

The advice above may seem a little out of your comfort zone, but remember that once you have stabilized your finances, built up a three- to six-month household cash expense reserve, and matched your employer's maximum contribution to your retirement plan, you can begin to wisely add back some luxuries and acquire whatever assets the King allows you to purchase.

Do-It-Yourself

Let's take a look at some areas where you can make an immediate difference in your finances by doing the work yourself.

Do Domestic Chores

Have you fallen into the habit of paying others to do your

domestic chores and projects? My painter was recently too busy with other customers to come and paint a door for me, so I went to the home improvement store, bugged everybody that I could find, including another customer, and finally left with all the supplies and how-tos I needed. I had never painted anything before, so I was a little intimidated at first. But the door turned out great, and the only cost I incurred was for materials. It was a very rewarding experience. Further, I made a simple, no-sewing-required window treatment using yards and yards of rich-looking but inexpensive fabric. I have received many compliments on it.

I'm ready to tackle anything now. I'm like the man who some-one asked, "Can you play the piano?"

"I don't know," he said.

"What do you mean you don't know?"

"Well, I've never tried."

You'd be surprised at what you can do if you try. Every day I experience Philippians 4:13: "I can do everything through him who gives me strength" (NIV).

Do you wish to spruce up your house but have no funds to do so? An entire television show and website (www.dyi.com) is dedi-cated to showing you the details of every facet of remodeling and home repairs. Further, your local home improvement store most likely offers how-to classes.

Beyond doing home projects yourself, you could also decrease the number of times your paid domestic services are performed. For example, why not stretch your housekeeper's service to every two or three weeks, or even once a month. You can change the linen, clean the showers, and vacuum the floors yourself. If you own a pool or Jacuzzi, request cleaning services less frequently, especially during winter months. And yes, you can remove leaves and cut wood.

Finally, do not forget to wash your car yourself. Enlist the help of your children, a relative, or a friend. What a great way to bond with someone. A thank you, such as a sandwich or a few dollars, will still be less expensive than the price at the car wash.

Understand that all of these sacrifices may be just temporary. You will be on solid financial footing soon and can gradually add back these services as your revised spending plan allows. The only goal now is to get out of the red and into the black.

Groom Yourself

You can save tons of money in personal grooming without sacrificing your appearance. Pay close attention to the techniques used by your various providers. Soon you will be able to do your own manicures, pedicures, eyebrow shaping, and other services.

Controlling Food Costs

Sometimes I wish God had made our bodies to require food only once a month or so. After all, He designed the marmot to hibernate for up to nine months. Imagine the time and money we would save. Since we can't avoid eating, those who desire to control their finances would do well to learn how to eat more economically. So here's my two-cents on eating in and dining out.

Guidelines for Eating In

Make a List. You can avoid unnecessary trips to the market by making a preprinted list of the items you buy regularly. Post a copy of it on or near your refrigerator. When you see that you are running low on an item, put a check mark by it. Don't forget to take the list with you to the store. After all my efficient planning,

I would often leave the list at home. Just when I would start to make macaroni and cheese, there would be tons of macaroni but no cheese. Neither to be outdone nor to waste money on gas for that extra trip, I used to get creative when I discovered I was out of a main ingredient in a dish I was preparing.

Pacify the Kids at the Market. If you cannot get out of taking the kids to the market, give them a "market allowance" of a couple of dollars or so to buy whatever they'd like. This is a great time to teach money management skills. Don't cave in to their begging for more money. Insist they spend within their budget.

Buy in Bulk When It Makes Sense. Some people take unit pricing to the extreme. They buy bulk quantities of certain items only to have them spoil because they never consume it all before it goes bad. Don't be penny-wise and pound-foolish. On the other hand, large families and those wishing to be frugal would be wise to stay away from convenient individual serving sizes and prepackaged items. I love coleslaw, but I refuse to buy the little 16-ounce ready-to-eat package. Rather, I buy a head of cabbage and shred it with my serrated knife. This yields about four times the prepackaged amount at a 75 percent cost saving.

Do the Standard Stuff. You know the rest: Don't go to the market hungry. You will likely spend more and buy things you don't need. I do this from time to time and often consume an item while shopping. When I get to the checkout counter, I give the clerk the empty package, look straight ahead, and say, "Charge me for this." I would be wise to have a snack before leaving home.

And yes, clip coupons. They are available all over the place now—Internet, coupon books, mailbox flyers, newspapers. Keep them in an envelope in the car. Even if you're not a subscriber to the local paper, it's worth buying the Sunday edition just to get the coupons. You really can save a ton of money doing this.

Cook in Bulk. In my effort to be health, time, and cost conscious, each week I devote a few hours to the kitchen and cook several of our favorite entrees at once. I then put them in meal-sized portions in freezer bags. I have also invested in a food-sealing machine, which allows food to be kept even longer in the freezer. My husband and I can each take a serving to work for lunch or have it for dinner. We simply add a salad or other quick side dish. This works great for beef, chicken, and fish dishes as well as soups, casseroles, pasta dishes, and beans. Don't forget to label and date the freezer bag with a marker; everything seems to look alike when it's frozen. Also, since our dinner prep time is shortened, Darnell and I have more time to talk to each other—that rare pastime that few couples engage in these days. Of course, we still eat out once or twice a week.

And speaking of cooking, try to take your lunch at least three to four days a week. Plan to eat out only one day at a fun place. This really is a healthier and less expensive route. I priced a made-at-home, top-quality turkey sandwich with natural chips and determined this lunch cost about 20 percent of the take-out version at a local eatery.

Guidelines for Eating Out

Eating out is enjoyable, but it can really blow your budget. When eating out, try the money saving strategies below to tame the cost of this increasingly popular pastime.

Predetermine Your Ordering Limit. When I take my staff out for one of our morale-building lunches, I give them a spending limit. Here's how it works. To determine how much you can order before tax and tip, simply deduct one-fourth (25 percent) off your total limit. If your limit is $20, take one-fourth off ($5) and limit your order to $15. When you add back the sales tax and a 15 percent tip, the total will be close to $20 without exceeding it.

Dine Early. Most restaurants will allow you to order from the less-expensive lunch menu up until late afternoon. This works especially well on the weekends. Call ahead or ask if this option is available.

Split a Meal. My husband and I will split an entrée 90 percent of the time. Depending on the serving size, we also split a salad and certainly the dessert. You'd be surprised how little it takes to satisfy your appetite. I'm just now getting it in this area. I was raised with a get-full, clean-your-plate mentality.

Stick to the Basic Meal. Skip the drinks and appetizers, unless you decide to make an appetizer your meal. Have the server bring it with the other diners' entrees, or they may feel free to help themselves to it. After all, it is an appetizer.

Ask for a Doggie Bag. Try to eat only half of your food and take the rest for a later meal. Your waistline will applaud you. Also, this gets you two meals for the price of one. If you don't eat the food within 24 hours, wrap it up and put it in the freezer for later. Don't let it go to waste.

You probably know most of the things I've suggested above, but sometimes it takes one more repetition of an idea for the light bulb to come on, and you finally say, "I'm going to do it!"

So, "Just do it."

Watch Wastefulness

Jesus set a great example of frugality. Even though He had performed a miracle and fed a crowd of 5,000 men and an undisclosed number of women and children with only five loaves and two small fish, He instructed His disciples to gather up the leftovers: "Now gather the leftovers, so that nothing is wasted" (John 6:12 NLT). When it was all said and done, they gathered 12 basketfuls.

Now, Jesus, you may wonder, *was that necessary? You could have thrown that extra bread away. All You had to do was perform another miracle and make more bread when You needed it.* Through His actions, Jesus showed the importance of not squandering what God has provided—even when it appears that you do not need the excess.

I talked to a couple recently who had lived a lavish lifestyle, but through a series of misfortunes had lost everything. They are starting to rebuild their lives and are working at jobs that pay much less than they were used to making. I asked them about the role they had played in their financial decline, and they confessed they were partly responsible. I concluded from a casual observation of their current behavior that a lot of their old wasteful habits were still alive and well. They called it "generosity" when they gave a 95 percent tip to the restaurant's parking attendant. By no means am I opposed to such bigheartedness, but when you're trying to stabilize your finances, frugality is a significant part of spirituality. God is not pleased when we engage in extravagance. Fortunately for some, during an economic downturn available credit is reduced or eliminated, which forces them to spend less.

In one of His parables, Jesus talked about a son who convinced his father to give him his inheritance before the appointed time. "A few days later this younger son packed all his belongings and moved to a distant land, and there he wasted all his money in wild living" (Luke 15:13 NLT). When the economy turned sour, he could only find work feeding a farmer's swine. He almost starved to death. At one point, he was so hungry he longed to eat the pods he was feeding to the swine. He finally realized that his father's servants were living better than this. He humbled himself and headed home. His merciful father was glad to receive him and gave him a big welcome back party. Of course, the father was by no means condoning his son's wastefulness, but rather celebrating his coming to his senses.

Are you wasteful in any area of your life, or do you actively seek ways to practice frugality? For instance, do you allow your children to open a can of soda, take a few sips, and then trash it? Did you know special lids are available at the supermarket that allow you to seal the can and preserve the fizz? Are you too embarrassed to ask for a doggie bag when you eat out? Do you bring home leftovers from the restaurant and then allow them to spoil in the refrigerator? Do you consider reusing plastic lunch bags, especially when you use them only for dry goods such as chips and cookies? They can be recycled at least once after a quick swipe with a damp towel. Do you always turn the lights off when you leave the room? Do you use both sides of the paper when printing drafts of reports—at home and at work?

I have practiced frugality as far back as I can remember. Darnell teases that I squeeze each dollar so tightly it's a wonder I don't rub George Washington's face right off the front. Yes, I turn the bottle upside down and get the last drop out of everything. I pick up every penny I find when I'm out walking. As Benjamin Franklin said, "A penny saved is a penny earned." I use vinegar and water instead of the fancy cleaners to clean glass and shiny surfaces.

I do everything I can to save money—not to hoard it, but so I can share it. I can't think of a single thing I have ever purchased that has brought more joy than writing a check to someone who desperately needs it. We are never more like Christ than when we are giving.

However, we should not allow our desire to be frugal to keep us from fully enjoying the things that are within the bounds of what God allows. I thoroughly enjoy the breathtaking view of the city from my home. My husband and I have made great sacrifices in putting the needs of God's house before our own desires. Therefore, we refuse to allow Satan to make us feel guilty about what God has provided.

Frugality is not a call to poverty, and it should not take the fun out of our lives. It is important that we enjoy the abundant life Christ came to give us. It is equally important to understand that abundance is not to be equated with extravagance. God blesses His children with abundance so they can bless others with their overflow. If we are all poverty-stricken, how will we have an overflow?

Frugality is simply avoiding waste. Wastefulness will keep your finances in a tailspin. Frugality is evidence that God can trust you with increased resources because you have learned how to manage what He has already supplied.

11

INCREASE YOUR SMARTS

We all know that knowledge is power and this is an information age. The financial survival of the fittest requires that you be in the know on several fronts.

Further Your Financial Intelligence

The financial illiteracy that pervades the country is alarming. U.S. Senator Mike Enzi said it best in his comments to the United States Banking Committee in February 2002:

> Financial literacy is something that is needed over a broad range of income levels. No matter how much one earns, money management is a necessity. It is something we need to begin emphasizing in grade school and continue all of the way through high school. It shouldn't stop there. Financial education should be something we continue to concentrate on for our entire lives.

Many times a person's finances have been derailed not so much from their disobedience to God's Word, but rather from a lack of knowledge about how to handle their money. I taught a six-week financial course for a small group composed mostly of young female college graduates. One of the students, bewildered by her low credit score, explained how she handled her monthly payments on her credit cards. "I don't pay on them every month," she said. "I just save up so that I can send in a really large payment. Is that okay?" I wanted to faint! Obviously she didn't know that her payment habits are one of the key components of her credit score. It is clear that many of our schools are not preparing students for the real world of finances.

Very few people invest in increasing their financial literacy. King Solomon admonished,

> Buy the truth, and do not sell it;
>   Also wisdom and instruction and
>   understanding.
>
> (PROVERBS 23:23)

It is extremely important that you empower yourself with some basic financial knowledge. Let's look at a few areas where this is key.

Car Leasing. In general, leasing a vehicle is not a good idea. However, if you are either in dire need of a car and have no money for a significant down payment or you work close to home and, on average, will drive less than 15,000 miles per year, leasing is an option you may consider. Before you sign on the dotted line, ask the dealer for a sample lease and then let some knowledgeable person explain the terms, especially "guaranteed residual value." This is the value you are guaranteeing the dealer the car will be worth at the end of the lease term. Because this value is determined primarily by how many miles you have driven, you can't just jump in the car and take a cross-country trip each year without penalty. My husband leased a car once, and we became prisoners to the odometer. "We'll go in your car!" he always seemed to exclaim. Of course, this caused us to rack up more miles on my vehicle, which we had purchased.

Business Deals. I advise getting professional help—especially legal and accounting expertise—when you're about to enter a business venture. Uncle Joe may be doing great at his small business, but he may not have a clue when you start talking about the nuances of profit-sharing agreements and exit strategies. Attorneys and CPAs are not experts in everything, so get one who specializes in your area of concern. It will be worth the investment.

Payroll Deductions. If you don't understand any aspect of your finances, then start asking questions. If you do not understand every deduction on your paycheck and know which ones are optional or subject to your control, then go to your payroll or personnel office and ask them to explain each one. You just may decide that you could improve the quality of your life by increasing your current deductions and taking home extra cash now rather than getting that large tax refund at the end of the year.

Upgrade Your Technical Skills

Anyone applying for an office job in today's technologically advanced age must be able to at least navigate the Internet and type a letter using Microsoft Word. I was appalled recently when interviewing candidates for a personal assistant position to encounter applicants who didn't have these basic skills. So let this be a friendly nudge to get with it. You don't necessarily have to spend time sitting in a classroom to get these skills. Just get a manual or log on to training sites on the Internet and stay focused. Keep inquiring, keep learning.

> Let the wise listen and add to their learning,
> and let the discerning get guidance.
> (PROVERBS 1:5 NIV)

In the workplace, learn other procedures and systems outside of your area of responsibility. It shows that you have initiative and an interest in the company. This could work only in your favor. Decide to like your job and be grateful that you have it.

Most studies show that the majority of people are not satisfied with their jobs. What makes many dissatisfied is their assumption that they have no other options. Others are not willing to invest the time, energy, and funds to learn additional skills or to venture out in their own business endeavor.

Pursue Your Passion

I challenge you to bring your passion to your work environment. You don't have to be self-employed in order to love what you do. I have held a few positions where I could hardly wait to get to the job to pursue my passion of implementing effective processes, negotiating difficult agreements, and solving whatever problems would arise. Problem solving is one of my passions. When others run from an issue as if escaping from a burning house, I can be found with the water hose running toward it.

Your passion will not go unnoticed and can result in financial gain. Of course, on a job you may not have the freedom to pursue your passion to the fullest, but if you maximize your experience there, it could very well be the springboard to realize your ultimate dream. Whether on the job or self-employed, Scripture admonishes us to be enthusiastic no matter what we do. "Whatever your hand finds to do, do it with all your might, for in the grave, where you are going, there is neither working nor planning nor knowledge nor wisdom" (Ecclesiastes 9:10 NIV).

Watch out for negative folks who try to put out your fire. Saboteurs of your passion are a dime a dozen. Some people simply may not share your passion for your area of interest, while others are just plain envious because your efforts remind them of what they could be doing. You have to treat such people as you would a toxic substance—minimize your exposure to them.

12

ACCEPT CHANGE

We are all creatures of habit, and most of us find it difficult to embrace change. But during times of economic uncertainty, we must be prepared to make concessions about our preferences and druthers—especially as they relate to housing or employment. It is important to remind ourselves that God is indeed our *source* and that He selects the *channel* through which He provides for us. Our jobs and other streams of income are *channels* for our resources. Further, our current residences are *temporary* dwelling places; we will not spend eternity there.

I am constantly reminded of the words of my spiritual mentor, the late Dr. Juanita Smith. She admonished, "Wear the things of this world like loose garments." This simple advice is hard to practice in our materialistic world where we work hard for and cling to our possessions. I have spoken to several people who were crushed when they lost their homes due to interest rate adjustments on their mortgages, unemployment, uninsured medical problems, or other misfortunes. Yet, others have taken the loss of their homes in stride. What makes the difference in their attitudes? I believe it's a mind-set that says, "Everything has a purpose. The will of the Lord be done!" rather than, "It's not fair!" It's all a matter of how much we trust God with our destiny.

Biblical Examples of Embracing Change

Let's look at the response of a couple of biblical characters who found themselves having to embrace change during an economic downturn.

Elijah the Prophet

When God instructed Elijah to declare a drought in Israel, Elijah soon realized that he too would be affected by the lack of food. However, being a man of faith, he knew that God is never without a channel.

> Then the word of the LORD came to him, saying, "Get away from here and turn eastward, and hide by the Brook Cherith, which flows into the Jordan. And it will be that you shall drink from the brook, and I have commanded the ravens to feed you there." So he went and did according to the word of the LORD, for he went and stayed by the Brook Cherith, which flows into the Jordan. The ravens brought him bread and meat in the morning, and bread and meat in the evening; and he drank from the brook (1 Kings 17:2-6).

Ravens! Those nasty birds will eat anything. They have a special fondness for dead animals and garbage. Yet God *commanded* them to bring His prophet two meals a day. We must be careful not to *despise* our channel when we are forced to take a less prestigious job, downgrade our housing, or make other life adjustments. Further, we must also be careful not to *depend* on our channel.

> And it happened after a while that the brook dried up, because there had been no rain in the land.
> Then the word of the LORD came to him, saying, "Arise, go to Zarephath, which belongs to Sidon, and dwell there. See, I have commanded a widow there to provide for you." So he arose and went to Zarephath. And when he came to the gate of the city, indeed a widow was there gathering sticks (17:7-10a).

Before you breathe a sigh of relief that he no longer had to be fed by the ravens, let me rush to tell you that this woman was not a rich widow but a single parent who—along with her son—was on the brink of starvation. Yet, she was the chosen channel that God had *commanded* (as He had commanded the ravens) to supply Elijah with food. Because of her obedience to God, the widow, her son, and the prophet survived and never ran out of food during the entire drought (1 Kings 17:10-17).

The Rich Shunammite Woman

This hospitable woman of great financial means willingly opened her home to Elisha, Elijah's protégé. She and her husband even added a room to their home to accommodate his frequent visits to their town. Although childless when she met Elisha, he prophesied that she would have a child and, much to her delight, the prophecy came true. (Elisha later restored her son to life after he suddenly became critically ill and died.) Life was good. That is, until God ordered a famine in the land, and she and her family found themselves having to relocate for their own survival.

> Then Elisha spoke to the woman whose son he had restored to life, saying, "Arise and go, you and your household, and stay wherever you can; for the LORD has called for a famine, and furthermore, it will come upon the land for seven years." So the woman arose and did according to the saying of the man of God, and she went with her household and dwelt in the land of the Philistines seven years (2 Kings 8:1-2).

Note her willingness to accept change. I'm sure I would have been tempted to respond, "Oh no, Elisha. I don't want to leave my beautiful home. Why, I finally have it decorated just like I want it. What will happen to it while I'm gone?"

I tend to be resistant to such major changes. However, I'm asking God to give me the grace to be flexible when I need to be so. I caution you to consider how well you accept change. If you're affected by a financial crisis, are you still bent on a certain course of action to your own detriment? Are you too embarrassed, too stubborn, or too proud to make a needed change? Are you willing to take a lesser position within your company or a not-so-prestigious part-time job at a fast food place or other humble place to close the gap in your income? Would a move to a smaller home or an apartment alleviate a heavy cash burden? Is your image more important than your survival?

You may have to accept a new role in the family, especially if you've been laid off. You probably never envisioned being "Mr. Mom," but what a wonderful opportunity to get a firsthand appreciation of what your multitasking wife has been experiencing all this time. Or maybe you're the stay-at-home wife who must now seek employment to close the gap in your income. Do it joyfully with a grateful heart that you have the ability to work. And what about your God-given gifts you could put to work right now with passion? Baking? Gardening? Sewing? Car detailing? Editing? It's time to get going. The money will follow your passion.

What change do you need to embrace? Victor Frankl, Austrian psychiatrist and Holocaust survivor, said, "When we are no longer able to change a situation, we are challenged to change ourselves."

When Change Challenges Your Integrity

During an economic downturn, your employer may find it necessary to reduce your pay. You may perceive this to be an unfair decision. One of the most powerful lessons on how to respond with integrity to an unfair employer is found in Genesis 29–31, the story of Jacob and his employer-uncle, Laban.

Laban subjected Jacob to all kinds of deceit and inequities. He tricked Jacob into marrying his not-so-attractive older daughter, Leah, after he had agreed to work seven years for the younger, more attractive Rachel. Jacob was forced to work another seven years in order to marry the woman he loved. Laban changed Jacob's compensation agreement ten times. Yet Jacob never lowered his standard of work in retaliation for Laban's unfair treatment. He later explained to his wives, "You know that I've worked for your father with all my strength, yet your father has cheated me by changing my wages ten times. However, God has not allowed him to harm me" (Genesis 31:6-7 NIV).

God instructed Jacob to leave the unfair situation and return to his homeland. He took his family and his hard-earned fortune and left without notice. When Laban heard about it, he gathered his posse and chased after him. However, before he could catch up with Jacob, Laban had an encounter with God, who told him to be very careful with what he said to Jacob. When Laban overtook

Jacob's party, Jacob confronted him with courage. "I have been with you for twenty years now. Your sheep and goats have not miscarried, nor have I eaten rams from your flocks" (31:38 NIV).

If you find yourself in an unfair situation, resist the temptation to "eat rams" from your employer's flock. Don't make personal long-distance calls, take supplies home, or take extended lunches. Continue to perform as if God were evaluating your work and watching your every move—because He is. Continue to seek His favor regarding a raise or simply seek employment elsewhere. Remember that no one can disadvantage you when you walk uprightly with the Lord.

> The righteousness of the upright delivers them,
> but the unfaithful are trapped by evil desires.
> (PROVERBS 11:6 NIV)

While God promises to open the windows of heaven and to pour out blessings on the person who tithes (Malachi 3:10), dishonesty will open the back door for those blessings to flow out and never benefit you. Your blessings will end up in pockets with holes in them. I have heard of people who faked injuries and received large legal settlements, only to wonder later where all the money went.

> A fortune made by a lying tongue
> is a fleeting vapor and a deadly snare.
> (PROVERBS 21:6 NIV)

Know that dishonesty can impact your entire family. When God allowed the Israelites to defeat Jericho, He told them not to take any of the spoil. But a young man named Achan took money and clothes and hid them in his tent. When his sin was discovered, he and his entire family were stoned and burned (Joshua 6–7).

Be careful not to set an example before your children of lying and cheating for financial gain. They will more than likely copy your behavior and fall into the same pit. One of the best legacies one could leave for his family is one of integrity.

> The righteous man walks in his integrity;
> His children are blessed after him.
> (PROVERBS 20:7)

Riches unjustly gained can never really be enjoyed and have no positive end. As Christians, we are commanded to walk in integrity. Integrity is simply the act of integrating what we say we believe and what we actually do. Yes, even professing Christians can have an integrity problem. When we fail in this area, others see it as a disconnect in our testimony. Many unsaved folks are turned off by such hypocrisy.

During economic uncertainty is a good time to search yourself and determine if there are any areas of your life where you may not be walking in integrity. Integrity also includes keeping your word. When people cannot depend on you to repay your loans or to show up when promised, they will not be inclined to extend any loans or bailout measures to you when you may need it most. Do not rationalize your behavior. Simply take whatever steps are necessary to slam shut this back door. I am reminded of the words of Job,

> He thwarts the plans of the crafty,
> so that their hands achieve no success.
> (JOB 5:12 NIV)

I have asked God to trouble my conscience so that I can't sleep, function, or proceed in any endeavor where I am not operating in complete integrity. Would you be willing to pray such a prayer?

13

CULTIVATE CONTENTMENT

A few years ago, overwhelmed with discontentment about the progress of my career, I went down to the Santa Monica pier to meditate and talk to God about my frustration. Despite the endless parade of tourists and the solicitations for money by the homeless people who gather there, the environment has a peaceful aura with its crashing waves and the beautiful mountain range that frames the coastline. I was especially perturbed this day having just learned that a colleague who worked in another industry had recently been promoted to a position that commanded a salary six times higher than mine. We had comparable educational backgrounds and it just didn't seem fair. A mutual friend who felt much envy toward what she thought was my idyllic life took great delight in sharing the news of my colleague's good fortune. Understand that I had no unmet needs, but hearing of Joan's (not her real name) new purchasing capacity made me feel disadvantaged.

After a couple of hours of whining to God, I gathered my beach chair and umbrella and headed for my car. There was a grassy stretch about 20 feet from my parking space where several homeless people were resting on their worn, smelly blankets. As I approached my car, a homeless woman who appeared to be in her early forties gave me a warm smile.

She's just trying to butter me up so I'll give her some money, I thought. To my surprise, she simply said, "Hi."

Wow, I'm going to get my purse out of the trunk and help this lady out.

I went to the car, grabbed a few bills, and headed back toward her. As I was about to extend my hand to say, "Here's something for you," I felt a check in my spirit. "Don't insult her dignity. Just talk to her," the still small voice said.

"Do you mind if I join you on your blanket?" I asked.

"Of course not," she said in a friendly tone as she gestured for me to sit down.

We talked for several minutes. I found out her name was Marsha, and I listened with great interest as she responded to my questions about the circumstances that led to her living on the streets and what her goals were for improving her condition. We had a wonderful conversation (my husband says I'll talk to a stop sign). When I finally arose from the blanket, I felt it was appropriate now to offer her the money I'd been clinching in my hand.

"Marsha, do you mind if I give you some money?"

"Oh, no, I don't need it," she said. "Give it to someone else. I have eight dollars. I don't take money out here if I don't need it. Besides, I have plenty of food."

She opened a medium-sized trash can liner to reveal an array of junk food—stuff I'm prone to eat when feeling stressed. The Twinkies looked really tempting.

"So many people out here have nothing," she said.

I felt two inches tall as I slinked to my pricey foreign convertible to drive home to a house overlooking the city. Here I had spent two hours whining, and this woman was content with eight dollars. What a lesson on contentment.

The Goal of Contentment

So when is enough, enough? Do you find yourself unable to enjoy what you have because your thoughts always seem to wander to what you don't have? Contentment should be the goal of every person who desires to walk in financial freedom. In our "more, more, more" society, anyone who is content is viewed by the stressed-out masses as lazy and without ambition. Various surveys show that people felt richer in the '50s than they do now with our bigger houses, HD TVs, low-calorie frozen dinners, cable TV, cell phones, and the Internet. Why is this so? I'd say it's because we're overwhelmed with trying to obtain and maintain too much stuff. Most people have not learned how to be content.

Benjamin Franklin captured our dilemma with his memorable words, "Money never made a man happy yet, nor will it. There is nothing in its nature to produce happiness. The more a man has, the more he wants. Instead of filling a vacuum, it makes one." Does this sound like the millions of home buyers who foolishly obtained loans they could not afford because their "eyes were bigger than their financial stomachs"?

Contentment in the Bible

The apostle Paul said that "godliness with contentment is great gain" (1 Timothy 6:6). We must understand that discontentment is a state of the *mind* in which we never feel satisfied with our present possessions. On the other hand, contentment is a state of the *heart*. A contented child of God says, "Father, I thank You for everything I am blessed to have right now, and I rest in Your promise to give me the desires of my heart and to meet every need I have according to Your riches in glory. You see the financial goals I've submitted to You. I receive Your grace to do all that I am supposed to do, and I leave the rest to You."

You will gain great joy and satisfaction once you decide that enough is enough.

Now, to be content does not mean to be complacent. A complacent person is satisfied with his circumstances and desires no more. A child of God who is content is satisfied that his material needs have been met, and any future needs will be met on a planned delivery schedule and at the appointed time. We must understand that God has always worked on a set timetable. He sent His Son to the earth "when the fullness of time had come" (Galatians 4:4). He promises to exalt us "in due time" (1 Peter 5:6). We must stay surrendered to God's sovereign schedule.

It is no wonder, then, that the apostle Paul exclaimed that godliness with contentment is great gain. One who has achieved this level of spiritual maturity has gained the victory over anxiety and the gravitational pull of worldly materialism.

Antidotes for Discontentment

Let's look at a couple of antidotes for discontentment.

Gratitude. One of the key steps to slaying discontentment is to become grateful for everything. Take nothing for granted. At the end of each day, take a few minutes to remind yourself of every provision God has made for you and your family that day. Did you have transportation to work today? Did you have a choice of what outfit to wear? Were you able to obtain the food you wanted? I'm reminded of the words of a popular song we used to sing in church, "Count your blessings, name them one by one. Count your blessings, see what God has done." Commit to making this a habit.

Solid Relationships. A key factor in avoiding the pitfall of discontentment is to become more relationship focused and less stuff oriented. When we read about the Shunammite woman to whom Elisha wanted to express his appreciation for adding a room onto her home for him and his servant, we immediately sense her contentment:

> Then he said to Gehazi his servant, "Call this Shunammite woman." When he had called her, she stood before him. And he said to him, "Say now to her, 'Look, you have been concerned for us with all this care. What can I do for you? Do you want me to speak on your behalf to the king or to the commander of the army?'" She answered, "I dwell among my own people" (2 Kings 4:12-13).

Even though she was barren, she had made peace with her plight. She had not focused on what was missing in her life, but rather on what she had—meaningful relationships. She was not concerned with climbing the social ladder. She had no need for anyone to speak to the king on her behalf, thank you. She had found contentment in her relationships. Many people will spend thousands of dollars to go to faraway places and interact with strangers they will never see again rather than investing time in building meaningful relationships at home.

The Shunammite woman had the wisdom to say, "I'm content

with what I have." While she was blessed with enough abundance to build a room for the prophet, nothing suggests that she was in pursuit of more. She was content to serve God and to honor Him with the resources she had been blessed with.

I know a couple that made a deliberate and wise decision to pursue a simpler lifestyle in order to spend more time with their two teenage children and family. I am certain they would like more possessions, but they have chosen to avoid the stress and the relational consequences of trying to acquire and pay for more, more, and more. They have said, "We have enough." Consequently, they are much more creative in their social activities, and an aura of peace surrounds them. Their more stressed-out peers seek their company as a haven from the never-enough-stuff madness that permeates our society.

Jesus gave a strong warning to His disciples, and it is still appropriate: "Beware! Guard against every kind of greed. Life is not measured by how much you own" (Luke 12:15 NLT). The ability to be at peace with our current possessions is a spiritual and emotional discipline that will probably be a lifelong quest. Even the apostle Paul said contentment was something he had to learn: "Not that I speak in regard to need, for I have learned in whatever state I am, to be content" (Philippians 4:11). Contentment is learned behavior; it doesn't happen overnight.

Contentment is not just about becoming frugal, for we can spend less but still be discontented in our heart because we'd like to spend more. However, an attitude of gratitude will go a long way toward solidifying our peace of mind.

Part 3

Beyond Financial Survival

14

COPING PSYCHOLOGICALLY WITH UNCERTAINTY

Even though advice abounds on how to cope financially during hard economic times, it is equally important that you cope well psychologically. Of course, how you cope psychologically is closely related to your belief system, which as a child of God is rooted in your faith. Unfortunately, as a result of the economic crisis, many people are plagued with hopelessness, irritability, and anger.

It has been widely reported in the media that telephone help lines, psychiatric offices, and other mental health outlets are strained to capacity. People are unable to cope with their shattered dreams and inadequate financial resources. Through it all, there is refuge in the Word of God. "So there is a special rest still waiting for the people of God. For all who have entered into God's rest have rested from their labors, just as God did after creating the world. Let us do our best to enter that place of rest" (Hebrews 4:9-11 NLT).

Let's see how to get to that place.

Finding a Place of Rest

Meditate on the Almighty

The faith walk can be tough. It violates your sense of logic to grasp that God is all powerful, all knowing, everywhere present, and wants the best for you. Nevertheless, you must maintain this perspective to enter into His special rest. If you allow your negative circumstances to supersede these truths, anxiety will become your constant companion. It's a decision you must make throughout the day—with every newscast, every credit card bill that arrives, every layoff, every delinquency notice, and everything that shouts negativity. God is still in control.

As you meditate, put forth your petition. Hear yourself acknowledge your inability to solve your problem in your own strength. This develops your humility and reminds you of your dependence on God. He already knows what you need. "Therefore do not worry, saying, 'What shall we eat?' or 'What shall we drink?' or 'What shall we wear?' For after all these things the Gentiles seek. For your heavenly Father knows that you need all these things" (Matthew 6:31-32).

We cannot escape life's troubles or stressors, but we can fortify our spirits with prayer and the Word of God so that we can have the strength and courage to respond to and overcome them.

Focus on the Bright Side

Developing and maintaining a positive outlook requires not only faith, but also mental discipline. While you may believe that God is in control of your life, often the reality of a situation can overwhelm your mind and threaten to negate your faith. In times like these, it pays to have developed the habit of "casting down imaginations, and every high thing that exalteth itself against the knowledge of God, and bringing into captivity every thought to the obedience of Christ" (2 Corinthians 10:5 KJV). As you arrest negativity, "fix your thoughts on what is true, and honorable, and right, and pure, and lovely, and admirable. Think about things that are excellent and worthy of praise" (Philippians 4:8 NLT). Resist the urge to bring God down to your reality; bring your thoughts up to His power.

The amount of stress that you experience in a situation will be determined by your attitude toward what is happening. If you start confessing that you are overwhelmed, then you will experience what you have heard, for faith comes by hearing—and so does doubt. Therefore, if you maintain that God is in control and that you will prevail, indeed you will. Begin to act as your own "attitude police."

Connect with Your Support Base

Everybody needs a support system. No one should attempt to deal with financial or other pressures in isolation. I believe that isolation is one of Satan's most effective strategies. He has a clear shot when there is no one to help you block his fiery darts. "A person standing alone can be attacked and defeated, but two can stand back-to-back and conquer. Three are even better, for a triple-braided cord is not easily broken" (Ecclesiastes 4:12 NLT).

I knew a young lady who had a baby out of wedlock. She also had a very demanding job. Unfortunately, she had no support system. She did not have a warm and friendly personality, rarely extended herself to others, and had not invested in the kind of relationships where people were aware of and willing to help her when problems arose. She often found herself in a dilemma when her child needed to be picked up from day care or required other special attention when she was not able to get off from work. King Solomon admonished, "A man who has friends must himself be friendly" (Proverbs 18:24).

I know firsthand the value and benefit of support when I'm under stress. Not only do I have a supportive husband, but I also come from a large family who will come to my rescue at the drop of a hat. Beyond just having someone to commiserate with about the problem, it's great to know that person cares about the outcome. Study after study has shown that people who have caring support live longer, recover from illnesses faster, and find life more meaningful. Support gives us a sense of connection and acceptance that are core human needs. It is an arena where you can be vulnerable, a place where you can feel safe saying, "I don't know," "Can you help me?" and "I need a hug." This is support God's way.

In the ideal world, our primary support would come from our family. However, if this is not your reality, don't despair and don't get stuck wishing it were so. God has made provision for you through small groups at church, people with common sports or professional interests, coworkers, and other groups. You must take the initiative to reach out and establish meaningful relationships.

As you seek to solidify your support system, keep in mind that support must be mutual. "Share each other's burdens, and in this way obey the law of Christ" (Galatians 6:2 NLT). Nothing is more detrimental to a support system than for it to become one-sided. Don't become so engulfed in your own issues that you forget that your supporters are also dealing with pressures. Inquire about and genuinely listen to their concerns. Nobody likes a taker.

I had a friend who could not listen to my issues for more than a few minutes before she would interrupt and turn the conversation into an endless discussion of her problems. I pointed out to her several times her tendency to do this, but she never changed. It was so frustrating. I finally became "too busy" to continue the relationship.

Finally, don't forget to express tangible appreciation for those who support you. Cards and token gifts on special occasions go a long way in saying, "I acknowledge and appreciate your help." Don't allow your support system to fall apart because of lack of nourishment. God doesn't want you to walk on the dangerous ground of isolation.

Laugh

The impact of laughter on stress is well documented. Studies show that it lowers blood pressure, reduces stress hormones, and cleanses the lungs and body of accumulated stale air. It boosts immune functions in the body. In addition, laughter triggers the release of endorphins—those chemicals in the brain that make you feel joyful and elated. These are the same chemicals released when some people, after an extended period of running, get "runner's high."

Being merry is a choice. No one can force you to be merry by saying, "Just be happy!" When the Israelites were taken captive by the Babylonians because of their disobedience, they lost all desire to play their musical instruments.

> We put away our harps,
> hanging them on the branches of poplar trees.
> For our captors demanded a song from us.
> Our tormentors insisted on a joyful hymn:
> "Sing us one of those songs of Jerusalem!"
> (PSALM 137:2-3 NLT)

Your ability to laugh and to be merry is often a good indicator of where you are in your relationship with God. The Israelites had lost their connection with God.

> But how can we sing the songs of the LORD
> while in a pagan land?
>
> (PSALM 137:4 NLT)

Your stressful lifestyle can take you so far from God that you feel you are in a "pagan" or "foreign" place spiritually and unable to laugh and find joy in the things that once caused you to be merry.

Humorous situations surround us each day. We just have to be on the lookout for them and not ignore them. We should take advantage of every opportunity to have a good hearty laugh. Swap jokes with friends. Let people know that you enjoy a good laugh. Don't be shy about sharing your most embarrassing moments (let good taste prevail here). Laugh at your mistakes, especially on the job. Be a good sport. When others do imitations of you, laugh and pay attention. It can be a real eye-opener to some of your eccentric ways.

Don't allow life's pressures and negative circumstances to snuff out your sense of humor. Laughter is a positive emotion and makes you a lot more fun to be around. Nobody enjoys a sourpuss. Laughter can also take your mind off what's stressing you. Laugh often, for the joy of the Lord is your strength.

Remember these words,

> "You will keep him in perfect peace,
> Whose mind is stayed on You,
> Because he trusts in You."
>
> (ISAIAH 26:3)

15

COPING RELATIONALLY WITH UNCERTAINTY

Marriages and other relationships can buckle under the stress of uncertain economic times. Try the strategies below for surviving your relationship with family, friends, and people in the marketplace.

Stay in Sync with Your Spouse

Even in the best of times, money can be a sensitive and conflict-ridden issue for many couples. Financial issues are the number one reason for failed marriages in the United States. Staying in sync with your spouse is critical in uncertain times. Failure to agree on the top financial goals and the strategy for achieving them can derail an otherwise good relationship. "Can two walk together, unless they are agreed?" (Amos 3:3).

Most couples would do well to understand the nature of a business partnership and to model certain aspects of their marriages accordingly. In a business partnership, the partners must practice full disclosure of financial information. There is no hiding of assets or details of transactions. Each partner agrees to the goals and objectives and has a say in all aspects of the enterprise.

When the Shunammite woman desired to build a guest room for the prophet Elisha, she didn't immediately call the contractors without getting her husband's input. "She said to her husband, 'I know that this man who often comes our way is a holy man of God. Let's make a small room on the roof and put in it a bed and a table, a chair and a lamp for him. Then he can stay there whenever he comes to us'" (2 Kings 4:9-10 NIV). Neither the fact that she could afford it nor the fact that it was for a good cause kept her from consulting her husband. He obviously agreed to the idea, for the next thing we read is that Elisha is settled into the room.

What a great lesson for women today, especially women who command their own resources. Many believe that no man is going to tell them what to do with their money. What a relationally destructive attitude. In a business partnership, everything that comes in belongs to the partnership. Marriage is a partnership on the highest order. In marriage there is no need to keep track of the financial contributions of each partner because no one should be anticipating a dissolution or final distribution of these funds, as in a business partnership.

Every couple needs to be in agreement on their major purchases. "Major" will be different for each couple depending on their household income. Each couple must decide the maximum amount that each may spend without consulting the other. Any amount above this will require complete agreement. Stick to what has been agreed. Trust me, this is important. If you don't get in agreement, should the deal go sour the tendency is to point fingers.

Many years ago Darnell and I purchased a spanking new recreational vehicle so we could camp out with our friends. Darnell convinced me it would also double as his regular transportation since he worked only a few miles from our home. Further, he sold me on the idea that since it could hold quite a few people, I would have loads of fun as he chauffeured all of us around town. We enjoyed a year of bliss with our new addition.

Things began to sour when Darnell's company parking lot was taken over for a construction project. Finding a parking space on the street became more of a challenge each day. It was clear that he needed a regular car. As with most vehicles, the RV lost a significant chunk of its value right away. We had financed it and found ourselves owing more on it than it was worth. The issue soon became, "Whose idea was it, anyway?" I silently pointed the finger.

We sold it at a huge loss and chalked it up to experience never to be revisited—until we bought the cabin cruiser several years later. I convinced Darnell that it would give me an opportunity to rest more and would even be a writing haven. Further, I would spend lots of time hanging out with him at the marina. He finally agreed.

When someone warned us that BOAT stood for "Break Out Another Thousand," we laughed. It turned out to be no joke. By the time we paid the monthly note, slip fees, divers to keep the barnacles off, insurance, and never-ending repairs from our infrequent usage, we started to wonder about our financial sense. Even though we both had agreed to the purchase, we apparently forgot to invite God to become a partner in the transaction. So once again we found ourselves owing more than the market value. We threw in the towel and decided to sell.

I am so gun-shy now that I'm limiting my recreational purchases to tennis shoes and sun visors.

The moral of these stories is to not only spend in harmony with each other, but also to get in sync with God. At least we can say that we didn't violate our rule for consulting each other on major purchases. It's just that we place such a high premium on harmony that we were not really honest about how we felt.

I have endless stories of couples that made big financial decisions completely out of harmony with their spouses. In one situation, the husband decided to quit his job for an entrepreneurial pursuit without consulting his wife. He announced his decision at a couples' fellowship as she sat there in shock and disbelief. She divorced him shortly thereafter.

In another situation, a Christian man who runs a business with his wife admitted that he has misled her into thinking they have a lot less money than they do. He says she's too financially irresponsible. "Besides," he rationalizes, "I'm the one who does most of the work anyway. She contributes very little." He thinks he has the right to buy several expensive toys while limiting her to what he deems a generous allowance. She resents him deeply for this. Rather than doing the difficult work of getting to the root of her financial irresponsibility, he chooses to deal only with the symptoms. The last I heard, they were still at odds but smiling in church every Sunday as if everything were all right.

If you and your spouse are experiencing financial problems, invite God to come into your partnership and give you the courage, the humility, and the wisdom to have an honest discussion about your money. Share in a nonemotional manner your expectations, disappointments, and desires about your finances. Start from the present; finger-pointing about the past is a useless exercise. Bring everything out of hiding, including old, destructive attitudes. Listen attentively to what your spouse says and make every effort to appreciate his or her viewpoint. Encourage your spouse to be open and sincere by being "safe" to talk to about the issues. You demonstrate that you are safe to talk to when you resist the temptation to judge, minimize, or pooh-pooh your spouse's ideas and opinions just because they may not be consistent with your own.

When my husband explained to me that work is a means to an end for him, I initially felt frustrated since I think that everyone should find joy *in the process* of working. I have learned to appreciate his mind-set and to benefit from his more balanced need for fun and recreation.

If the family breadwinner has experienced a cutback or layoff, make every effort to understand his (or her) frustrations and feelings of inadequacy. Assure him that he is more important to the family than a paycheck, and don't spend time whining about or reminiscing about the luxuries you've had to give up. Men, for goodness' sake, don't withdraw and go into a shell. Talk to your wife and family. Talking is therapy. Ever wonder why women live longer? Continue to be the head of your household by leading your family in prayer about your financial crisis and having the courage to set new spending guidelines and implement new core values. This is a legacy that will outlive all the stuff you could struggle to buy.

Stop Enabling Family and Friends

When your finances are strained is a good time to stop your enabling. One of my brothers swears that he would be much further along financially if we had not spoiled him by enabling him to be irresponsible for such a long time. He's right. Because he was the youngest of seven children and my mother and father separated during his early years, we all wanted to make sure he didn't miss out on what life had to offer. One of his older brothers became his surrogate father and bought him all kinds of expensive toys. He was often the envy of other neighborhood kids. As he grew older, he would borrow money from the family and faced no consequences when he failed to pay us back. He even joined a Corvette car club and didn't own a Corvette—he knew my car would be available. I spent a few weekend nights without transportation while he was cruising with his fellow car club members. That was more than 30 years ago, and I had never heard of the word *enabler*.

Enabling negative behavior can keep you in a financial pit. Mothers are among the biggest enablers. Many of them excuse the unacceptable behavior of their children, especially their adult sons. The scenario is the same in most families; only the names change. No matter how much the other siblings protest, Mom steadily bails the son out and declares that she knows him better than anyone else. After all, they have a unique relationship.

Some grandparents are also enablers. I remember an 83-year-old widow coming to my office in tears because she had cosigned for a car loan for her grandson, who had defaulted on it. Further, she had purchased auto insurance for him, and he was involved in an accident where he was at fault. The victims sued her and won. She was now being forced to sell her real estate to pay their claim. She was devastated. "I shouldn't have done it," she moaned.

Generally, it's a bad idea to cosign a loan for anybody, be it family members or friends. A person who needs a cosigner is a high credit risk or the lender would not require the security of another person's credit. The Scriptures declare,

> It's poor judgment to guarantee another
> person's debt
> or put up security for a friend.
>
> (PROVERBS 17:18 NLT)

This is not to say that you should never help your responsible sons or daughters when they are in need. However, if you cannot afford to lose the money, think twice. Once you've been stung by somebody's default, wisdom will set in quickly.

When people enable their children, spouses, or anyone else to remain irresponsible by bailing them out or always being their safety net, they interrupt one of God's most effective teaching tools—sowing and then reaping the consequences. Real maturity occurs when people learn their lessons through experience. Enablers also hinder a person's spiritual and emotional development as well as jeopardize their own financial security. That's poor stewardship.

What about you? Let's see if you fit the profile of an enabler.

- Do you have a special relationship with an irresponsible person?
- Do you try to protect him from the criticism of others?
- Do you make most of the decisions for this person because you know what's best and must shield him from negative consequences?
- Do you perform any tasks for this person that he could learn to do himself?
- Do you like feeling needed by this person?

Sometimes you can be so fearful of being rejected or alienated that you will enable your boomerang, able-bodied adult child to move back home with no financial responsibility. If your finances have been affected by your own enabling and you really don't have the heart to say it stops today, then start with a small thing to work your way out of the hole. Assign your adult child a utility bill, then the phone bill, next a small amount for rent. Have him buy his own food or whatever will cause him to take some responsibility. This is real love. The Scriptures will back you up on this. "Even while we were with you, we gave you this command: 'Those unwilling to work will not get to eat' " (2 Thessalonians 3:10 NLT).

This is a prime time to expose your children to the household budget. Straining your finances so they can keep up with others in their wardrobe, recreational activities, or other pursuits sends the wrong message. You're teaching them to live the same lies that have kept you in financial bondage. Get real with them about what you can and cannot afford and stick to your guns. I thank God a million times that my father did not spoil me and my six siblings. Whatever he doled out to us was final; there was never a renegotiation for more. We saw him budget every penny, and we lived pretty well compared to our neighbors and friends. Plus, he always had money to assist those who came knocking at our door for a helping hand.

A period of economic uncertainty is a good time to ask God to give you the strength to say no to all requests from irresponsible people in your life—from family members who always need "a few dollars" to freeloading friends who never have their share of the bill when you eat out. Heed the apostle Paul's admonition, "Each one should carry his own load" (Galatians 6:5 NIV).

Control Your Socializing Expenses

Here's a common dilemma. You enjoy the company of friends or coworkers who are big spenders and who always want to divide the restaurant bill equally. You sit there and stew because your share should be only $20, but it's now $50 because of their drinks, appetizers, and desserts—none of which you have ordered because you're on a budget or a diet. You don't want to be a cheapskate, but these outings can cause you to blow your entire lunch budget for the week.

If the bill-splitting dilemma is a recurring problem for you, try this strategy next time. Ask for a separate check before the server takes the orders. If this is not possible, grab the bill first when it arrives. Determine your share, plop down that amount in cash on the table, and excuse yourself to the restroom. If you're really secure, forget the restroom and just explain that your financial consultant (that would be me) has you on a spending plan so that you can achieve certain financial goals. Don't assume that anyone will think less of you. You may start a revolution on how a few others handle their finances.

If you really want to stick to your guns, leave your wallet in the car and take with you only enough cash to cover your spending limit. I've done this before. When they'd start the splitting routine, I'd say, "I brought just enough cash to cover what I knew I would spend."

Don't let splitting the bill cause you to stop socializing with friends and coworkers. Just be assertive without any drama and keep having fun.

Rethink Your Gift Giving

It seems there is always a holiday or special day of observance that requires us to buy a gift for somebody. My husband, though a generous man, says it's a conspiracy of the floral industry. I've heard others say it's a creation of retailers. Whoever can be blamed as the source, we still feel the pressure to buy a present for the honoree.

When I reviewed our spending recap one year and realized how much we spent on gifts, I decided it was time to pare it down. I looked through the list of recipients and realized we had purchased some of the gifts reluctantly or in response to the expectations of others. Some of the wedding gifts were for people we hardly knew. Many of you have most likely found yourselves in this dilemma.

A few years ago I came out of the supermarket one night and was approached by two ladies who asked for directions to the nearest bus stop. Noticing all the shopping bags they were carrying, I was curious as to how far they had to go. When they told me their destination, I realized it was not far from my house, and I offered to take them home. They accepted with great delight.

I found out they were both on vacation from Belize. I also learned that most of the bags belonged to just one of them and were filled with gifts for people back home. The shopping queen then began to complain that she had to buy all these presents or people would be disappointed because she always brought gifts back from the United States. She confessed she couldn't afford them and was distraught that she was forced to continue this costly habit. Further, she had spent a significant part of her vacation looking for the gifts and was physically drained as a result. She had started to dread the annual vacation because of this. There was no cheerfulness in her giving. I spent the next half hour advising her on ways to get off this roller coaster. When I asked the other lady how she had managed to avoid this gift-giving burden, she simply said, "I just don't do it."

I have seen many people create a financial monster they never have the courage to slay. I'm not recommending stinginess, but if your cash flow is strained during uncertain times, you must forge some brave new disciplines. I know that for some people, especially those with low self-esteem, going cold turkey and just saying "no more" will be too much. So I recommend that all financially challenged folks buy smaller and different types of gifts. For example, for the Belize shopper, I would suggest a postcard packet of Los Angeles key sites rather than a T-shirt and cap.

Wedding presents for distant acquaintances could consist of a set of good quality white bath towels, dish towels, a nice skillet, or other useful, generic items purchased from a super discount or closeout store. Forget about the bridal registry and the fancy place settings. This isn't mandatory. Also, forget about a cash gift. They won't guess that you paid only $10 for a $40 value, but a $10 cash gift looks (and is) cheap. If you stick to something useful, it will still be appreciated. Also, don't try to deceive recipients by putting the gift in a fancy box from an upscale store. They may attempt to exchange it, only to learn it wasn't purchased there. Tacky, tacky, tacky!

Besides, what statement are you trying to make with your gift anyway? Think about this long and hard and be honest. Are you living a lie by implying that you can afford such generosity? Are you trying to gain favor with the recipient? Do you know that favor comes from God and it's free?

> For surely, O LORD, you bless the righteous;
> you surround them with your favor as
> with a shield.
>
> (PSALM 5:12)

When it comes to those special days of recognition, you don't always have to send expensive flowers—except maybe on Valentine's Day. (Even then, your wife or girlfriend should understand a pared-down version.) Focus daily on being thoughtful; that will mean far more than a one-day obligatory observation. Valentine's Day is just a formality in our house. I'm more impressed with Darnell's love for me when he insists on taking all the grocery bags out of the car, washes dishes, fills my car with gasoline when it gets low, takes my car to the car wash, attends conferences with me to help promote my products, and shows overall consideration. To me, these are the best "flowers." Of course, being a woman, I do expect *something,* but I am satisfied with a single rose and a card.

Speaking of flowers, a nice plant is appropriate in many situations and will last longer and may cost less, especially if you pick it up and deliver it yourself, which is a nice touch in this rush-rush society. I just recently threw out a seven-year-old plant that friends gave us for a relative's funeral. It was a nice reminder of his life. A floral arrangement would have wilted within days.

Other pared-down presents include white handkerchiefs for men, movie tickets, a magazine subscription, nice stationery, note cards, or a book. None of these will send your budget spiraling out of control. I buy generic gifts (bath and body products, etc.), gift bags, and an assortment of special occasion cards a couple of times during the year and keep them in a special drawer. If I discover an upcoming birthday, I can assemble an inexpensive, thoughtful gift bag in minutes. It really is the thought—rather than the thing—that counts. I remembered someone and went to some extra effort to let him know it. If a person can't appreciate a gift unless it's expensive enough to put in escrow, then I question the authenticity of that relationship.

Christmas gifts pose the greatest challenge—all for no long-term benefit. What were the three most memorable gifts you received for Christmas last year? Can't remember? The people you gave gifts to have the same problem. So, if the gifts are not that easily recalled, why put yourself in a position of having to remember them each month when you make that credit card payment? Why give a gift that keeps on costing? Instead, give something simple from your heart. I was thrilled this past Christmas when a couple gave me a bag of personally concocted hot drink mix. They sealed it in a plastic storage bag and stuffed it in a gift bag with lots of tissue. It was so good that I coaxed them into giving me the recipe. I remember them every time I make the drink.

When you get to the point where your finances are stable and you're enjoying abundance, give according to your ability and your desire—and do it cheerfully. "You must each decide in your heart how much to give. And don't give reluctantly or in response to pressure. 'For God loves a person who gives cheerfully'" (2 Corinthians 9:7 NLT).

Improve Your Relationships in the Workplace

Cutbacks, reduced operating budgets, added workloads, office politics, long commutes, and other factors increase tension in the workplace and can keep you in a negative state of mind. Now is the time to rise to another level in your emotional maturity and your communication skills. You would be well served to assume that *everyone* is stressed. Therefore, give every offense the benefit of the doubt and respond calmly to daily aggravations. Remember that this is the "best of times" for the child of God, your finest hour to show His power in your life. Decide now that you are going to be the icon of peace no matter what happens.

If you work for a company, tighten up your act. Perform all duties with excellence; submit to your boss with a good attitude; be a team player. Don't be a clock watcher; arrive a few minutes before the regular start time and leave a few minutes later than the regular stopping time. Don't steal from your employer by doing personal work on company time or taking supplies home. Why sabotage your blessings? Make yourself indispensable, the last person to be considered for layoff. However, don't operate in fear and don't resort to backstabbing and other worldly ways of making yourself look good at the expense of another. Relax. Your destiny is in God's hands and nobody can thwart it.

> The LORD of Heaven's Armies has spoken—
>> who can change his plans?
> When his hand is raised,
>> who can stop him?
>> (ISAIAH 14:27 NLT)

For sure, you'll want to shore up your relationship with your boss. Give her your feedback and opinions with respect, but submit to authority as if you report directly to God. If the buck doesn't stop with you, simply learn to say okay to any request that is not illegal or immoral.

Enough said.

16

COPING PHYSICALLY
WITH UNCERTAINTY

Physical activity is an excellent stress-buster and is critical to normalizing your body after a stressful event.

When your brain senses a threat or danger, it quickly releases hormones carrying an urgent message to the adrenal glands (which sit atop the kidneys). The message says, "Let's prepare to resist or to run—now!" The adrenal glands produce excess stress chemicals, cortisol and adrenaline, and rushes them into the blood stream where they get delivered to various parts of the body. The body responds with increased strength, raised blood pressure, and all other assistance needed to resist or run. Countless stories tell of people who exhibited unusual strength in a crisis. I heard of a petite young mother who lifted the back of a car her child had been trapped under.

Of course, a crisis is not limited to threats of physical danger. The threat of losing a job or a loved one, or even the excitement of a happy occasion can cause the brain to put the body on high alert. The adrenal glands do not distinguish between negative or positive excitement.

Once the crisis is over, the excess hormones need to be dissipated out of the bloodstream. Regular physical activity helps to burn these extra chemicals so your body can return to normal. Imagine their buildup if you are under stress day in and day out. Studies have linked an accumulation of stress hormones to strokes, heart disease, high blood pressure, thyroid malfunction, decrease in muscle tissue, obesity, impaired memory, and a host of other maladies. And some people have died from heart failure in a crisis because their heart muscle was not strong enough to handle all the stress hormones pumped into the bloodstream.

In addition to its positive impact on stress, physical activity provides numerous other benefits including better resistance to illness, stronger bones, more energy, and stronger muscles.

What activity is best? The best form of exercise is the one that you enjoy and that you find convenient. These are the two biggest reasons most of us fail to follow an exercise program.

First, we lose interest in the activity because we don't get a lot of satisfaction out of it. I've had beginning lessons in almost every sport—at least two or three times for some. Rollerblading, skiing, swimming, golf, and even the Los Angeles marathon have not held my interest. I'm just a plain walker. I get great joy from bonding with my friends as we power walk or even stroll along beaches or through various parks and neighborhoods.

Second, we tend not to be consistent in an activity if it requires too much time or effort. Why join a gym across town and show up only two or three times a year? Exercising already requires discipline, so why allow inconvenience to add more stress to the process?

Whether a brisk walk or a high-energy fitness class, almost any physical activity will help you let off steam, distract you from your source of stress, and improve your mood. It also relaxes and reenergizes your body. Aim for a minimum of 30 minutes of physical activity a day at least five days a week. Doing more is even better. Some fitness gurus suggest that if you cannot carve out 30 minutes at a time, grab 10-minute segments throughout the day.

There are other benefits to making exercise the center of your stress-blasting program. Active people tend to eat better, and a healthy diet also helps your body manage stress better. In addition, physical activity can help you lose weight and keep it off, which make you feel better about yourself. Feeling physically inadequate can be a stressor in itself.

If you cannot find the time for an official workout, try building the activity into your lifestyle. My doctor suggested that I park on the outskirts of the shopping mall so I'll be forced to walk farther. You may try taking the stairs several times during the day for a certain number of floors.

Stress can wear you down mentally and physically; however, a healthy body can cope with stress better than an unhealthy one. Jesus was adamant about His disciples taking time to rest and regroup from their activities. When they returned from their evangelistic tour and excitedly reported the successes they had achieved, Jesus did not respond with an "attaboy" or a "keep it up." Instead, "He said to them, 'Come aside by yourselves to a deserted place and rest a while.' For there were many coming and going, and they did not even have time to eat. So they departed to a deserted place in the boat by themselves" (Mark 6:31-32).

Jesus knew that if His disciples failed to shut down periodically for rest and recreation, they would become ineffective. We must stay on guard and understand that Satan wants us to go from one extreme to the other—all work or all play.

I observed during my years of financial counseling that women are more prone than men to overworking without recreational breaks. I'm guilty also. Further, when men play, they are more likely to engage in more expensive activities and feel no remorse about the impact they may have on the family finances. Be honest. Are you one of those people who insists on engaging in "champagne" sports without regard to your "Kool-Aid" budget? Can you really enjoy only golf, skiing, boating, and other high-cost activities? Do you find the idea of eliminating or cutting back on these sports unthinkable?

If you want to control your out-of-control finances, there can't be any sacred cows or off-limit activities. You simply must take a hard look at your spending plan and see how often you can reasonably indulge in these upscale activities. Keep in mind that you are a steward of the resources God has entrusted to you and that He will extend to you as much money as you prove you can handle.

I know a man who played golf with the guys several times a week while his house was in foreclosure and he had delinquent outstanding personal loans. His financial house was falling apart. He was frequently absent from work because of his recreational indulgences and was ultimately fired for his poor attendance. I can explain his behavior only as an addiction or just plain irresponsibility.

Whatever happened to jogging, bike riding, swimming, and other low-cost alternatives? Do you really have to meet your friend for breakfast, or would a brisk walk better serve you both while you catch up on each other's lives? For most of my close friends, I now ask that our get-togethers consist of a walk on the beach or around the local high school track rather than facing that irresistible basket of bread at our favorite restaurant. We save money and calories.

As you look at restructuring or downsizing your recreation, keep in mind that it should refresh you mentally, physically, or both. The word *recreation* implies that new life is imparted in the process. Thus, your choice of recreational companions is as important as the activity. Engaging in pleasurable activities with pleasurable people maximizes the value of the recreation.

My husband tries to play golf only with guys he really enjoys. He says the camaraderie is an integral part of the activity. I have noticed that a walk with an insecure, competitive person increases my heart rate and puts a damper on my day. On the other hand, when I walk with a woman who loves God, who is pursuing her goals in life, and who knows how and when to listen, I feel energized. Many times the walk turns into a season of prayer or, at other times, just gut-level laughter that "does good, like medicine" (Proverbs 17:22).

Restructuring your recreation may mean that you pass up the popcorn at the movies. Did you know that movie theaters make more profits from concessions sales than from admissions? Consider making your own popcorn when you get home at a fraction of the cost. This would also be a great time to critique the movie and to bond with your mate or date. After all, no conversational bonding happens during the movie.

I'm sure you can name loads of things you can do to spend less on recreation. Take a moment and commit to at least one thing you can do right away. Whatever you do, don't cut recreation out completely. To survive and thrive during a financial crisis, you must exercise financial discipline in every area possible.

CONCLUSION
In God We Trust

Weeping may endure for a night, but joy comes in the morning" (Psalm 30:5). What a relief to know that trouble doesn't last always. Economic downturns do end eventually. During times of uncertainty, we must allow the Holy Spirit to work the fruit of patience in us so that we can endure temporary adversities and allow them to press the best out of us. We must resist becoming frustrated and fearful.

As I was counting the cash in my wallet recently, I was at once fascinated and challenged by the inscription that appears on the back of each bill: "In God We Trust." It seems ironic that in reality, many have placed their trust in the currency and have forgotten the essence of the motto. Does this describe you? Is your trust in your currency or in your God?

Yes, the purchasing power of the dollar and stock values may fluctuate, but that should not present a cause for alarm. As we embrace and walk out our faith, we can be assured that trusting in God will always bring us more stability and power than any denomination of money. Let this fact loom large in your mind.

Face the Facts with Faith

The story of Abraham inspires me. He had the unique ability to face facts but not allow them to diminish his faith.

> And Abraham's faith did not weaken, even though, at about 100 years of age, he figured his body was as good as dead—and so was Sarah's womb. Abraham never wavered in believing God's promise. In fact, his faith grew stronger, and in this he brought glory to God. He was fully convinced that God is able to do whatever he promises. And because of Abraham's faith, God counted him as righteous (Romans 4:19-22 NLT).

The man was 100 years old with a 90-year-old wife, yet he believed they would still have their own son—and they did.

Have you ever run into a situation in which all the facts were stacked against you? Several years ago when my husband and I decided to "move up" from our first home, the price of the house we had set our hearts on was out of our predetermined range. Our goal for wanting to move was to be closer to our church so that we could serve the ministry more effectively. We were growing weary of the commute. I had long desired to have a home with a view of the Los Angeles skyline. What a sight that is with beautiful mountain ranges set as a backdrop. The church was only minutes away from a very hilly neighborhood with awesome views. Our pastor, the late Dr. H. Marvin Smith, told us not to limit God to our budget on this transaction because we had been faithful in our service and our stewardship. We found a house we fell in love with and made an offer on it. The seller immediately rejected it. We did not feel led to increase the offer, so we said, "The will of the Lord be done."

A few weeks later, the seller relented but demanded a 10 percent deposit within a few days. We had 1 percent in hand. God strategically had my very unsupportive, immediate boss leave town during this period. I worked for a Fortune 500 company at the time and had favor with the corporate treasurer's administrative assistant. When I appealed to him for a temporary loan until we could sell our existing home, he approved it immediately—without a set due date or collateral. This was nothing short of a miracle. After overcoming numerous other roadblocks that threatened to derail the purchase, we finally moved into the house and enjoyed many years of rich fellowship with our church members, family, and friends. It was truly God's house.

I can recount an endless number of other situations where it looked as though the facts would thwart my financial blessings. I even went to graduate school on a fellowship and earned a master's degree in business finance from the University of Southern California—after being told that I was rejected due to my low score on the entrance exam. I told the Lord, "You're going to look really bad because I've been confessing for the past six months that I was going on a leave of absence from my job to go back to school." I was so disappointed that I went to Europe and spent the money I had saved for school. However, God was working behind the scenes. One month before school was to start, they informed me they had changed their minds and would be granting me the all-expenses-paid-plus-a-stipend fellowship. I didn't know whether to cry or shout. I was so financially motivated that I finished the two-year program in seven months!

We must never allow facts to overshadow our faith. The Bible is filled with stories of faith overriding facts. Peter, James, and John were calling it a day after fishing all night with no success when Jesus came along and instructed them to try again. Now, if the fish were not biting at night, surely the daytime was the worst time to expect any results. Nevertheless, they ignored these facts, acted on Jesus' word, and experienced a miraculous, net-breaking catch (Luke 5).

Have you allowed certain facts to dash your financial hopes? Does your FICO score place you among the "undesirables"? Is your debt ratio outside of your bank's traditional lending range? No down payment? No collateral? Not enough time on the job? No credit history at all? Is there a desperately needed item outside your budget? Are you going to succumb to these facts, or do you have the faith to ask God for a miracle? Know that just as people major in certain subjects in college, God has a major also. He majors in impossibilities.

It's a lot easier to exercise faith when you've been obedient. Long before Abraham received the son he was promised, he had a history of obeying God. When God got ready to bless him abundantly, he told Abraham to leave his pagan-worshipping relatives and to relocate to some not-yet-determined place that God would show him. There is no evidence that Abraham even hesitated (see Genesis 12). He obeyed immediately. He responded in a similar manner when God told him to offer Isaac, his long-awaited son of promise, as a sacrifice. He obeyed without question, and God found a substitute for the sacrificial offering (Genesis 22). What a model of faith!

Each time I have needed divine intervention in a financial transaction, I have been quick to remind God of His promises to the faithful. Because faith comes by hearing, I memorize His promises. I write them on the back of old business cards to recite when walking. I put them in picture frames to keep in view during the day. I type them in large fonts, post them on my treadmill, and say them out loud. This builds my faith and takes the teeth out of the fears generated by the facts.

I try to keep in mind that "faith is the confidence that what we hope for will actually happen; it gives us assurance about things we cannot yet see" (Hebrews 11:1-2 NLT). In the words of my friend Dr. Judy McAllister, "The more faith you have, the less evidence you need."

What facts are you facing today? Believe the Word of God and don't let the facts overshadow your faith.

Just C-O-P-E

I pray that what I have shared in the preceding chapters has given you not only hope, but some practical strategies for navigating the financial uncertainty in your life. Using the word *cope* as an acronym, let me reiterate the actions I want you to take now.

Chill. This colloquial term means to relax, to cease worrying. It's easy to become so overwhelmed with the enormity of a situation that you start chasing your tail to do something about it. God says to His children,

> Don't worry about anything; instead, pray about everything. Tell God what you need, and thank him for all he has done. Then you will experience God's peace, which exceeds anything we can understand. His peace will guard your hearts and minds as you live in Christ Jesus (Philippians 4:6-7 NLT).

In other words, calm down. God is not pacing the floor in heaven trying to figure out how to avert a financial tsunami. He is writing history. Therefore, we have an awesome opportunity to show the world our faith by how we respond to the chaos that surrounds us. Our peace should be so evident that others will want to question us regarding it.

God's children have no need to join the line of those seeking anti-anxiety medications. This is not an indictment against those who genuinely need such medications due to chemical imbalances and so forth. But it is an indictment of our faith to be anxious—to anticipate a negative outcome—when God has promised to meet our every need.

As negative financial reports are broadcast over the airwaves several times a day, I remind myself—often out loud since faith comes by hearing—that God has never forsaken those in right standing with Him. No need to panic, to pull money out of the bank and put it under the mattress, to take on a zillion part-time jobs in anticipation of lack. Let your prayer closet become a place of refuge and mental refreshing from the unending barrage of negative news. Stop and release all your fears and frustrations to God, whether sitting in stalled traffic or sitting in a meeting that seems to be going nowhere. When I begin to feel overwhelmed, I have made it a practice to go into a dark room, lift my hands, and say out loud, "I cast all my cares upon You, for You care for me."

Obey. It is critical that we remain obedient in our giving and helping those in need. Proverbs 3:9 says to *honor* the Lord with our possessions and the *first* fruits of all our increase. Be careful not to *dishonor* God by putting Him *last* on your financial priorities list.

Further, a financial crisis is not the time to become fearful or selfish when it comes to helping those in need. The widow of Zarephath, on the brink of starvation, moved beyond her fear during a severe economic downturn and sacrificed for Elijah. As a result, she, her son, and the prophet experienced an inexhaustible food supply until the crisis ended (1 Kings 17:8-16). Know that you will indeed reap a reward for every seed of generosity that you plant in the lives of others.

Not only is it critical to obey the leading of the Holy Spirit in your giving, you must also seek His guidance in how you handle the rest of the resources He has entrusted to you. Be on guard against wastefulness, cutting moral corners to make ends meet, enabling those who are irresponsible, and other behaviors that sabotage your finances.

Plan. Plan to get out of debt as quickly as possible. Plan how you will accumulate your emergency reserve. Plan your future; tomorrow is only a day away. Plan time with others; going into isolation is not going to improve your situation. It makes you a target for depression and all kinds of mental attacks. In times of uncertainty, you need a solid base of support, so plan to nurture your relationships. Plan an exercise routine to take care of yourself physically. If you have been laid off, plan to read all the books and other materials you've been storing for when you had idle time.

Plans give you purpose and focus. Know that while you are making plans, God has a few plans of His own for you. " 'For I know the plans I have for you,' says the LORD. 'They are plans for good and not for disaster, to give you a future and a hope' " (Jeremiah 29:11 NLT).

Expect. Do not rest your hope or expectations on governmental or other solutions to the crisis. Rather, expect God to work on your behalf. Be reminded of the admonition in Psalm 62:5 (KJV): "My soul, wait thou *only* upon God; for my expectation is from him." Our primary expectation must be of God.

I have drawn an imaginary horizontal line in my mind that separates the "sense" realm from the "faith" realm. I am determined not to be moved by what I see or hear. The just live by faith! I learned in my high school physics class that no two forms of matter can occupy the same space at the same time. To me, this has profound spiritual application: it is impossible to dwell on negativity while focusing my thoughts on the promises of God. So my strategy is to *feed my faith and starve my fears.* How do I do it? By reading and reciting the Word of God; by speaking words of hope and victory versus doubt and defeat; by listening to television programs that inspire faith, limiting my exposure to negative newscasts; by seeing the present uncertainty as a temporary event; and by making every effort to remain obedient to God in every area of my life. I challenge you to do the same. My peace has certainly surpassed my understanding.

I challenge you to get excited about the miracles God wants to work for you—especially if you have been (or have decided to be) obedient in your giving. My own experience bears this out. When my husband's employer reduced his work week to half time for over a nine-month period, we could have fed our fears. After all, his income was the bread and butter of our budget. Being in full-time ministry, my income cannot always be projected as it consists primarily of speaking fees and royalties from my book sales. However, by the grace of God, my books have enjoyed strong sales. I'm happy to report that during the season of reduced employment, every obligation was met in a timely manner. We did not resort to credit card debt nor drastically adjust our lifestyle. To boot, we continued to maintain cash reserves at a level we never seemed able to achieve when we both worked in lucrative executive positions. Consistent with God's faithfulness, the extra time that my husband was available allowed us to pursue—at our own pace and discretion—another income opportunity we had been resisting due to our busy schedules. To God be the glory.

God honors His word. He is not wringing His hands trying to figure out a solution to individual, national, or international financial dilemmas. He is simply looking for a nation or a person who will come boldly to His throne and receive His help. "For the eyes of the LORD run to and fro throughout the whole earth, to show Himself strong on behalf of those whose heart is loyal to Him" (2 Chronicles 16:9).

You can C-O-P-E during these perilous financial times and continue to experience God's peace. Let Him show Himself strong in your life. Pray without ceasing. Here is a prayer to get you started.

> Father, I rejoice in the truth that you supply all my needs according to Your riches in glory (Philippians 4:19)—without regard to my paycheck or other expected channels of income. I need this truth to be evident in my life and financial situation now. Your Word assures me that those who seek You will not lack any good thing (Psalm 34:10). I resist anxiety about my current shortfall in resources. I know that You do not want me to be anxious about anything, but in everything by prayer and supplication, with thanksgiving, to let my requests be made known to You, and Your peace, which surpasses all understanding, will guard my heart and my mind (Philippians 4:6-7). I need Your peace now. My eyes are on You to fill the gap in my finances.
>
> I ask Your mercy and forgiveness for any disobedience, dishonesty, delaying, or any other shortcoming on

my part that has caused me to be financially disadvantaged. Help me to always put Your financial priorities ahead of my desires and wants, for Your Word declares that if I am willing and obedient, I will eat the good of the land (Isaiah 1:19).

Surround me with the favor that You promised for those who are in right standing with You (Psalm 5:12). I believe, according to Your Word, that You are able to do exceedingly abundantly above all that I ask or think (Ephesians 3:20). In the name of Jesus, I pray. Amen.

FREQUENTLY ASKED QUESTIONS

B elow is a summary of the questions asked most frequently by people trying to deal with the economic crisis. I attempted to address the most common concerns in the preceding chapters, and I hope the information below will further enhance your understanding. For more specific advice about your situation, please consult your financial professional.

Is my money safe in the bank?

Your funds are safe as long as your bank is insured by the FDIC. Here's the scoop in the agency's own words from its website at http://www.fdic.gov/news/news/financial/2008/fil08102a.html:

> The Federal Deposit Insurance Corporation (FDIC) is an independent agency of the United States government that protects against the loss of insured deposits if an FDIC-insured bank or savings association fails. FDIC deposit insurance is backed by the full faith and credit of the United States government. Since the

FDIC was established, no depositor has ever lost a single penny of FDIC-insured funds.

FDIC insurance covers personal and business funds in deposit accounts, including checking and savings accounts, money market deposit accounts, and certificates of deposit (CDs). It also covers retirement accounts, trust accounts, and various other types of accounts. FDIC insurance does not, however, cover other financial products and services that insured banks may offer, such as stocks, bonds, mutual fund shares, life insurance policies, annuities, or municipal securities.

In October 2008, the insurable limit was temporarily raised from $100,000 to $250,000 per *depositor* (versus per *account*) per bank, including all branches of that bank, through December 31, 2009. See www.Myfdicinsurance.gov or call 877-275-3342 or 703-562-2200 for details or changes to the insurable limit.

You may check the insurability of your account at your bank by going to http://www2.fdic.gov/EDIE/calculator.html. This site allows you to input general, non-private information about your account into a calculator to determine if you are within the insurable limit.

If you are fortunate enough to have funds on deposit in excess of the insurable limit, spread the excess over to other banks. Remember, the insurance applies to each bank.

What about the safety of my funds at my credit union since credit unions are not insured by FDIC insurance?

Your deposit shares in your credit union are insured by the National Credit Union Share Insurance Fund (NCUSIF) which is backed by the full faith and credit of the U.S. Government.

The federal government's bailout bill of October 2008 temporarily increased the insurance coverage from $100,000 to $250,000 per depositor through December 31, 2009, on all accounts.

NCUSIF is managed by the National Credit Union Administration (NCUA), an independent government agency. Credit Unions insured by the NCUSIF must display in their offices the official NCUA insurance sign. Not one penny of insured savings has ever been lost by a member of a federally insured credit union. Even state-chartered credit unions are required by some states to be federally insured. To confirm that your credit union is insured by NCUSIF, go to http://www.ncua.gov/indexdata.html. Deposits in 95 percent of the nation's state-chartered credit unions are insured by NCUSIF. American Share Insurance (ASI) insures 163 state-chartered credit unions (http://www.nascus.org/state-cu-facts.htm).

Where is the best place to park the cash I have for my emergency fund and extra savings reserves?

Now that you understand that your money is safe in your bank or credit union, surely you won't be tempted to keep any of it under your mattress or in your home safe. I do recommend, however, that you keep a good sum of cash on hand for unforeseen events. This amount should be determined by several factors, such as the number of people in your household who depend on your income or the number of cars your family drives. In areas prone to natural disasters such as hurricanes or earthquakes, ATMs may not work right away after a disaster. Therefore, you may need a cash reserve to purchase gasoline, food, emergency supplies, or even to give token amounts to those who help you in your distress. Keep the money in small denominations ($1, $5, and $10 dollar bills). Resist the temptation to use this stash for everyday needs just because you forgot to get cash from the ATM this week. (Okay, I'm guilty!) Remember, it's for emergencies.

The rest of your emergency fund should be kept in a money market checking account, interest savings account, or other account that can be accessed on short notice without a withdrawal penalty. Avoid putting the cash in a long-term instrument such as a two-year certificate of deposit (CD). Use CDs, short-term cash management funds, or floating rate funds for your longer term cash savings.

Should I withdraw from my 401(k) to pay off credit card or other debt?

Unless this move is necessary to save your life or that of a loved one, this is about the worst financial decision you could ever make if you are under 59.5 years of age. First, the Internal Revenue Service assesses a 10 percent penalty for early withdrawal. The penalty is payable when you file your annual income tax return. Second, you must include the amount you withdraw in your regular income for the year that you withdraw it. Third, if you live in a state that assesses personal income taxes, you must also include the withdrawal in your income for state income tax purposes. Finally, states with personal income taxes may also assess an early withdrawal penalty. Here is an example that shows how costly this move can be:

> Deborah withdrew $50,000 from her 401(k) plan to purchase a home for her aging mother. Being a CPA by profession, she was well aware of the penalties and other costs of her decision. When she filed her joint tax

return with her husband that year, she had to pay the following amounts for this transaction alone:

10 percent IRS penalty	$5,000
Federal taxes on the $50,0000 withdrawal	10,750
State (CA) 2.5 percent early withdrawal penalty	1,250
State Income Taxes on $50,000 early withdrawal	3,000
Total cost of transaction	$20,000

Only $30,000 of the $50,000 withdrawal was available for Deborah's use after all of the taxes and penalties. However, she spent the entire amount on the real estate transaction and had to pay the $20,000 in taxes and penalties from her savings.

So, if you chose to make an early withdrawal, you would be wise to hold back a portion for your impending tax liability rather than spend the entire amount of the drawdown. At a minimum, you might want to plan for 25-30 percent in taxes and early withdrawal penalties. If you are over 59.5 years of age, no penalties will apply, but you still must pay applicable federal and state income taxes. To avoid a tax underpayment penalty, deposit the taxes at the very next federal and state quarterly due dates using federal and state estimated income tax forms available online.

The example above is a true story. My story. The names have not been changed to protect the innocent, but rather left unchanged to educate the uninformed about the consequences of such an early withdrawal decision.

Instead of an early withdrawal, what if I just take out a loan on my 401(k)? Are the consequences the same?

Most 401(k) plans allow you to borrow up to 50 percent of your vested account balance or $50,000, whichever is less, for a maximum of five years—unless you are borrowing for a first home, which allows a longer payback. Tapping into your retirement nest egg is generally not a good idea; however, a loan is a better option than a withdrawal as you will not be assessed a 10 percent IRS early distribution penalty.

Sure it's easy, convenient, low-cost, and fairly hassle-free. The biggest downside is that the funds you withdraw are no longer being invested and earning money for your retirement. And the interest on the loan is not tax deductible. (If you are a homeowner, it's better to take out a home-equity loan, which allows you to deduct the interest on your income tax return up to a certain limit.)

Caution! If you don't pay back the loan on your 401(k), it will be treated as an early withdrawal with consequences like those explained in the previous question. If you leave your place of employment, you will likely be given a grace period of 60 or 90 days to pay back or arrange repayment of the loan.

Is it true that even though I pay my credit card bill on time each month, the credit card company could reduce my credit limit and negatively impact my FICO score? How so?

It is true that a reduction of your credit limit can impact your FICO score. How much debt you have outstanding determines 30 percent of your score. Here's how it works.

If you have a $2,000 limit on your Visa card and you owe $800, you are at 40 percent ($800/$2,000) of your limit. Not too bad; looks like you're exercising a lot of discipline. However, if the limit gets reduced to $1,000, and you owe $800, you are now 80 percent maxed out. Looks like you might soon head over the limit. This brings your FICO score down. And, yes, the credit card company can reduce your limit even if you always pay on time. Lenders are trying to minimize losses during uncertain economic times as more and more people become delinquent and default on credit card debt.

How long will a foreclosure stay on my credit record?

Seven years.

How long does a bankruptcy remain on my credit record?

The customary time a bankruptcy remains on a credit record is seven years. However, there is no law that prohibits a credit reporting service from keeping it on record after that.

I have large outstanding balances on all three of my credit cards, and I can pay only the minimum on one of them. The late fees and over limit fees have caused the balances to spiral out of control. What should I do now?

You must get help quick. Organize your bills and payroll check stubs (and other income documentation) and head for the nearest Consumer Credit Counseling Service center. They will explain how your situation affects your credit and how to manage your debts going forward. They will renegotiate your bills to an affordable level. You will pay them a lump sum each month, and they will forward payment to your creditors. Know that renegotiating your bills through a credit counselor will show up on your credit report and may lower your FICO score—but so will your continued delinquencies!

I'm behind on my mortgage, and I've gotten several solicitations from companies wanting to help me. I'm ready to get mortgage counseling, but I know there are scammers out there, and I don't know whom to trust. What should I do?

The Department of Housing and Urban Development (HUD) sponsors low- or no-cost counseling agencies throughout the country that can provide advice on defaults, foreclosures, buying a home, renting, and other credit issues. Using an interactive map, their website allows you to select a list of approved agencies for each state. Check it out at http://www.hud.gov/offices/hsg/sfh/hcc/hcs.cfm.

How do I pay off credit cards if I don't have a job?

Since you can't get blood from a turnip, you're going to have to get more creative and less selective about what you're willing to do to survive. Payoff does not have to be your top priority, but making the minimum payments should be.

You may have to swallow your pride and move in with a relative. Good communication is a must if you have to resort to this option. The arrangement should not be open-ended but have a termination date. Further, put the agreement in writing. If you cannot contribute financially at the beginning of the relationship, agree on other things that you can do (such as cook, wash cars, babysit, care for elderly parents). Make your presence in the household an asset. Don't just sit around running up utility bills; look for work every day. Inquire about and obey house rules, refrigerator boundaries, and so forth.

It's amazing the number of conflicts that can arise when a new person comes into an environment. Remember that everyone is already settled into a routine and you will probably be a disruption on some level. Commit to being a pleasant disruption. Pray for wisdom to flow with the other people in the household, and then just use common sense and do unto others as you would have them do unto you—in everything.

What is Ginnie Mae and how does it differ from Freddie Mac and Fannie Mae?

The Government National Mortgage Association (GNMA), nicknamed Ginnie Mae, is a U.S. government corporation within the Department of Housing and Urban Development (HUD). Unlike Freddie Mac and Fannie Mae, Ginnie Mae is not a publicly traded company. Ginnie Mae does not issue, sell, or buy pass-through mortgage-backed securities, nor does it purchase mortgage loans. It simply *guarantees* (insures) the timely payment of principal and interest from the banks, savings and loans, or mortgage bankers that issue the original mortgages. Most of the mortgages sold as Ginnie Mae mortgage-backed securities are those guaranteed by the Federal Housing Authority (FHA), which are typically mortgages for first-time home buyers and low-income borrowers. Unlike Freddie Mac and Fannie Mae (which went into conservatorship by the government in late 2008), Ginnie Mae's securities are backed by the full faith and credit of the U.S. government.

How does the Federal Reserve Bank figure into bank operations?

The Federal Reserve Bank (the Fed) makes loans to banks at a "federal funds rate." This ensures the flow of credit, which is the lifeblood of the economy. The Fed adjusts its rate periodically to control economic growth in the U.S. When the economy grows too fast, inflation results and people make fewer purchases. The demand for housing, goods, and services decreases. Eventually, prices will go down because people will have less disposable income. Thus, inflation is held at bay. Conversely, when interest rates go down, making purchases more affordable, the demand for housing, goods, and services rises and drives prices up.

APPENDIX 1

The Mortgage Cycle

(See Reference Notes for Explanation)

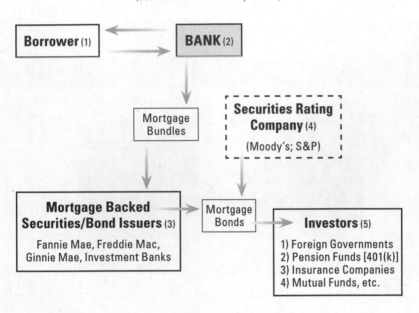

Reference Notes:

(1) Borrowers obtain loans from the commercial bank to purchase homes. Borrower makes down payments to the bank. The mortgage loans are secured by the related property.

(2) The commercial bank will sell a majority of its mortgages to Fannie Mae, Freddie Mac, or an Investment Bank ("bond issuers"). The bank may warehouse a few

of the mortgages at its discretion, but retains no interest in the ones that are sold. Bank may retain loan servicing rights making the transaction invisible to the borrower. Monthly payments from borrowers are sent to the bond issuers.

(3) Fannie Mae, Freddie Mac, or an Investment Bank will purchase a bundle of loans from the bank, repackage them into various bond categories depending on the risk and terms, and sell them to Investors.

(4) Before the bonds can be issued to Investors, they must be certified as "investment grade" by a securities rating firm such as Moody's or Standard and Poor's.

(5) Investors purchase the "rated" securities with the expectation of receiving the stated rate of return from Fannie Mae, Freddie Mac, the responsible Investment Bank, or an insurer who has guaranteed the bonds against default.

APPENDIX 2

My Balance Sheet
(What I Own and What I Owe)

As of _____
(date)

Assets (What I own)   **(Market Value)**

Cash in Banks   _____

Stocks and Bonds   _____

Cash Value of Whole Life Insurance Policy   _____

Jewelry/Art/Clothing   _____

Vehicles   _____

House/Condo   _____

Rental Property   _____

Retirement Fund   _____

Other: _____   _____

Other: _____   _____

                        Total Assets   [   ]

Liabilities (What I owe)

Credit Card #1: _____   _____

Credit Card #2: _____   _____

Credit Card #3: _____   _____

Auto Loan   _____

Mortgage Loan   _____

School Loan   _____

Other: _____   _____

Other: _____   _____

                        Total Liabilities   [   ]

        Net Worth (Assets minus Liabilities) [   ]

APPENDIX 3

My Income Statement
(What I Get and Where It Goes)

Month Ending _____

Take Home Income (After Taxes):

Source 1: _____

Source 2: _____

Total Income _____

Less: Tithes/Offerings (_____)

Less: Savings (_____)

Net Cash Available

FIXED EXPENSES

Rent/Mortgage _____

Property Taxes* _____

Auto Loan/Bus Fare _____

Auto Insurance* _____

Credit Card Payment: _____

Credit Card Payment: _____

Water/Gas _____

Electricity _____

Medical/Life Insurance _____

Total Fixed Expenses

* These expenses occur at irregular times. Simply take the annual amount and divide by 12 to get the amount you should set aside each month.

DISCRETIONARY EXPENSES

Auto Repairs/Maintenance   _____

Lunches   _____

Groceries   _____

Recreation/Cable   _____

Laundry/Dry Cleaning   _____

Telephone   _____

Gasoline   _____

Clothing   _____

Grooming (Hair/Nails/etc.)   _____

Vacation Reserve   _____

Other: _____   _____

Other: _____   _____

Total Discretionary Expenses   [_____]

TOTAL EXPENSES   [_____]

NET EXCESS (DEFICIT) CASH   [_____]

Appendix 4

Tracking Your Discretionary Expenditures

Week:_____	Mon	Tue	Wed	Thu	Fri	Sat	Sun
Gasoline							
Auto Repair							
Car Wash							
Snacks/Coffee (A.M.)							
Snacks/Coffee (P.M.)							
Lunch							
Dinner Out							
Groceries							
Recreation							
Manicure/Pedicure							
Cell Phone							
Telephone							
Gasoline							
Clothing							
Dry Cleaning							
Hair							
Cosmetics/Toiletries							
Other:							
Other:							
Total Expenditures							